BEHIND THE
SCENES

SARAH ALONGE

The events and conversations in this book have been set down to the best of the author's ability, although some names and details have been changed to protect the privacy of individuals.

Copyright © 2020 by Sarah Alonge

Published by Truthful Taboos Publishing
London, England
www.truthfultaboos.com

First paperback edition August 2020

Book design by Urban Stamp Graphics

ISBN 979-8-6710-6628-9 (paperback)

BEHIND THE SCENES

DEDICATION

This book is dedicated to God, the One who made it possible to tell my story and to every person who has experienced heartbreak. There is light at the end of the tunnel.

ACKNOWLEDGMENTS

I would like to thank God for his continued faithfulness and strength. Without it, this book would not have been possible To my parents Gbenga and Arinola Alonge thank you for your love and support. Mummy you held me up when I couldn't stand, you prayed for me, wiped tears away and supported me through it all. I couldn't have asked for a better mother than you. Thank you. Daddy you reminded me of my value. You made me feel like the most beautiful girl in the world and taught me to never settle for less. I love you. To my dear brothers Christopher and Charlie – thank you. More than brothers you are my friends.

To my spiritual father Bishop David Onimisi, thank you. From your continued encouragement, prayer and guidance, I appreciate you and the entire SICC family.

To my amazing pastors Rev Dana and Rev Wonu. Thank you. You reminded me daily that with God, there was no storm too big. You kept me accountable and never allowed me to stay down too long. To my friends, there are too many of you to mention. Thank you for everything. For being my community, my support system. But this book will not be complete without mentioning my sisters of almost 2 decades. Otega, Chingy and Stephanie you taught me what good friends should be. Because of your friendship, I have been blessed. My sisters who stood with me in adversary, I will always appreciate you.

BEHIND THE SCENES

PROLOGUE

21.

They say it takes 21 days to form a habit. I soon learnt that this is true.

I heard these words 21 days after I waited to hear from you. It was the first thing you said to me before everything changed.

I patiently waited, hoping that our love would win. I told myself that it was ok because that's what a good woman is supposed to do. A good woman waits even when she doesn't know how long she will be waiting for. She overlooks the emotional torture and the nights she spends crying, pleading and praying that it will get better.

At least that's what I thought a good woman should do.

For 21 days, I reminded myself of the memories that we shared. Our first date in 2010 was a memory stuck on replay. I can still feel the butterflies in my belly that were fluttering out of control as I embarked on the two hour train journey from Birmingham to London. I remember looking in the mirror countless times to make sure my hair was still laid, and my lipstick was still intact while constantly checking the time; only for me to realise only three minutes had passed since I last checked.

I anticipated how you would react when you saw me and how the scent of your cologne would make my knees quiver. As the days passed, I reminded myself of the nineteen year old girl with a crush that would soon blossom into love.

For 21 days, I relived our very first Valentine's Day together. I spent hours reminiscing on the suspense leading up to the evening

1

you planned for us; a memory I treasured.

You were always the most romantic man in the room. No matter how much I tried to guess what you had planned, I never could. I remember leaving church with you that evening and driving to your house. You made me believe it was a pit stop before heading out to the date you had planned for us. I was so giddy that I just wanted you to rush in and rush out while I waited in the car.

Luckily, I was in desperate need of the bathroom, so I jumped out of the car and as you opened the door, I looked down to see my feet serenaded in rose petals.

If I close my eyes now, I can still see candle lights on each corner of the room and smell the aroma of the three-course meal you made specially for me. It was the night you made me feel like the luckiest girl in the world.

And for 21 days, I thought about the first time you held me by the neck, leaned forward and kissed me.

For every one of those 21 days, I held on to the 5 years and 6 months that we shared; 2, 006 days. But still, I was left with 21 cold and lonely days.

The memories were all I had to keep me hopeful that chapter 21 was just a glitch on the long road we were embarking on to our forever.

It's funny to think that once upon a time, we would sit down and argue about the number of children we would have. You wanted two, which came as no surprise to me. You were always a man who liked the ideal setting. We would have one of each. Preferably a girl first and then a boy a few years later. We would move to the outskirts of the city and buy a house with a back garden and a front porch. But of course, I wanted three: two boys and a girl. I eventually managed to convince you that you wanted three kids too. And before we knew it, all three of our unborn children had names and personalities. Knowing you, this was probably your way of making me feel like I was in charge. Your way of doing whatever it would take to put a smile on the face you once referred to as the most beautiful face in the world. That is the you I chose to remember.

It wasn't long before I began to imagine telling our love story to our kids. It would be the tale of how two madly in love youngsters never gave up despite all the odds. And oh, there were many. We would tell them that when all hope seemed lost, we kept fighting. Always getting back up right after being knocked down. This would be the story we would tell them every time they considered quitting one of the many extra-curricular activities you were keen on enrolling them on to. It would be our way of emotionally blackmailing five and seven year olds to never give up but mostly our secret weapon to get them to do whatever we wanted.

For 21 days I waited. And on the 21st day, when you finally returned my call, I knew from the tone of your voice that our picture-perfect life was just that. A picture.

There was an uncanny feeling, like I was speaking to a stranger that I knew all too well. The unfamiliarity of the words coming from a voice so close. The voice that understood the look in my eyes and the thoughts of my soul. That once comforting voice became something I was afraid of.

As you began to speak, the world grew still. Your words to me on that faithful Thursday evening gave the number 21 a new meaning. It was no longer associated with the age of freedom, liberation and the beginning of something new. Now it represented the end.

21. That is the number of days you told me it took you to learn to live without me. By the 21st day you confirmed that there would never be another day of you and me. The words that followed are words that still haunt me. Words I never expected to hear from the man I grew to love and call my best friend. There were no pleasantries, no remorse in your tone. It was simple and to the point, your simple truth. And just like that, you told me:

"It takes 21 days to form a habit. It's been 21 days and I've been just fine. 21 days and I have survived. 21 days and Sarah, I know that for the rest of my days I can live without you."

At the tender age of 25 I faced the hardest challenge of my life to date. A challenge that put my life on display leaving it open to scrutiny, pain and pity.

For six years I dedicated my love, my time and my heart to a man that I thought was the love of my life. And within moments, my life appeared to come crushing down when in just a few short words, I realised that this relationship would never see year 7.

The years that followed consisted of a pain so deep caused by a love so close. I went through years of what the doctors clinically diagnosed as post traumatic anxiety. But really, I was suffering from a broken heart.

I remember hearing someone say that a broken heart is the worst kind of wound a person can go through; it is one with no clear timeline of recovery. And they were right. Each day I woke up wondering if this would be the day that I would finally stop feeling so broken.

Would I finally get a full night's sleep? But like clockwork, it was 3am and I found myself staring up at the ceiling while the silence of night gradually transitioned into the dawn of a new day.

I soon learnt that a pain so deep could only be comforted by a strength that transcended human comprehension. It was the kind of strength that would enable me to see that there was more to my life than a called off wedding and a bleeding heart. It would take me back to the time in my life that it all started. The girl I was before I met him, the girl I became when he found me and the woman I would grow into after he almost broke me.

It was the type of strength that would use what tried to break me to build me. And I was right. It was the strength that made me a survivor who went from existing to thriving.

It was that strength that gave my scars meaning.

PART 1

SCENE ONE:
THE BEGINNING

It was February 2010. I was approaching the end of my first year at university. So far, university had been an amazing experience for me. It was the first time I'd lived away from home and it was safe to say that a lot had changed. I acquired this new-found freedom that didn't naturally come to a Nigerian girl with age. In my case, it came with fleeing, or should I say sprinting away, from the nest.

Not having to check in on my location with my parents was a very welcomed experience in my life. Don't get me wrong, I had, and still have, an amazing relationship with my parents. But the regular texts of '*Sarah, where are you*' and the eavesdropping outside of my room door were two things that I certainly was not going to miss.

Like most, I received one thousand and one talks about how I should not bring my family name into disrepute whilst at university. I had a mother instructing me to 'face my books', a father reminding me to 'remember whose child I am' as well as aunties calling me from Nigeria telling me to 'make sure I keep my two legs in my trousers'. After politely responding with the 'yes ma' and 'yes sir' I took each word with a pinch of salt and began to plan how to make the most of my first experience living away from home.

Life from hence forth was for living and I planned to live my best 'care – free' life with no apologies.

My first term of university was exactly how I expected. Within the first week, I had made a few friends on campus and had visited all the hot clubs in Birmingham. The term consisted of late nights, house parties, learning the difference between gin and vodka and minimal studying.

I was having the time of my life.

Yet I failed to understand why I woke up each day unfulfilled; feeling like something was missing. It felt like there was an empty space inside of me. A void that I couldn't quite figure out or was satisfied with anything I was doing.

The end of our first term was fast approaching and the novelty of going out every weekend was beginning to fade away.

Me and my new friends Keji, Lola and Annabel decided to give nights out on the town a rest for a while. Keji was all too excited not to go out for the next few weeks and did not attempt to hide it. Of the four of us, she was the most likely to find an excuse to stay indoors. She once put in the effort of getting dressed, doing her makeup, only to fake a stomachache the moment the cab arrived! Lola was not any different. She was the typical case of *'I will get back to you'* which really meant *'no I am not coming'*.

Even though Annabel and I were out at almost every planned motive, the truth is, none of us were really party girls. We were simply four Nigerian girls taking advantage of our newfound freedom.

It had been three weeks since coming back to campus after the winter break. All over campus there were posters of an event advertised by the African Caribbean Society called the 'Valentines Special'.

Even though I had previously dated, I had never celebrated Valentine's Day.

Honestly, it was never an option. I have two older brothers and extremely protective parents. To them, a sentence that consisted of their teenage daughter having a boyfriend did not exist. If I so much as suggested that I was dating a guy, it would be world war three in my household. Of course, this just helped me to get creative on keeping whoever I was dating a secret. But there was no lie or story I could ever come up with that wouldn't raise suspicions if I attempted to leave my house on Valentine's Day.

As close as me and my mum were, we never spoke about guys.

The furthest we had ever gotten was 'no boyfriends until you finish university' and 'no sex before marriage'.

Culturally, this was not unusual. It was one of the many shared experience between Keji, Lola, Annabel and me. For us, going to this event on Valentine's Day was less about the day and more about the fact that we could go out without raising any alarm bells. So, we dusted off our going out shoes and registered to attend.

In England, February is always the coldest month of the year, so it was no surprise to us when it began snowing on the day of the event. Despite the weather, we took our time to make sure we looked gorgeous from our hair to our make; everything was laid to perfection.

Refusing to let the snow stop us, the girls and I decided to call a cab. But as we called each cab office in town, we were met with busy lines.

After 10 minutes of unsuccessful call, we finally got through to a local taxi company. But it wasn't great news. All taxis were backed up because of the snow. That year, the snow had reached record levels in over a decade. There were no buses running in the town, taxis were completely backed up and there was no way we would make it through the snow if we walked. Besides, we looked way too cute to be slipping, or worse yet, falling face front as we attempt to make our way across town.

Great! My first Valentine's Day away from home and bang! The snow came to steal my shine! Literally.

My friends decided to stay indoors but I was determined to go out. This Valentine's Day had to have meaning. It had to become something. I had to make it worthwhile!

The week before, one of the girls who lived in the accommodation across the way form me invited me to an event on campus called 'The Dating Game'. I know what you are thinking but stop right there. This was not a form of modern day blind dating, it was an event put on by a church on campus. I didn't want to go alone so I asked one of my housemates if she would come with me. Despite slight hesitation from her, she decided to come with me. I changed my heels for some snow boots and walked across campus.

***

I was excited to be going to this Christian event. I grew up as a Christian and for as long as I could remember, church was a big part of my life. I tried to find a new church when I moved to university, but nothing seemed to scream home to me. Before I knew it, I stopped trying to find a church and took advantage of my Sunday snooze fest after my Saturday night festivities. So, this unexpected change to my plans was one I was not too mad about.

Arriving at the lecture theatre, I was surprised to find the room was packed with so many students. The event had singers, a play, a sermon and more. My housemate and I thoroughly enjoyed it.

As the night progressed, I remember not wanting the night to end.

Suddenly, it hit me. That void that I felt, the emptiness that couldn't be filled with nights outs and social activities was suddenly being filled right in front of me. I had been missing God. The emptiness was being filled and I knew what I had to do; join a church.

A few weeks later, I officially became a member of the church and I loved every moment of it. I loved the new friends I'd made, my new strengthened relationship with God and the new joy I couldn't explain!

Of course, I shared this newfound love of God with Keji, Lola and Annabel. Before long, they too would occasionally attend the Wednesday mid-week services with me. But I was a regular. I became heavily involved in church service and I loved it. I swapped the gin with communion wine and my Sunday morning snooze fest to Sunday services. To look around the church and see my peers so passionate for God was something I was not used to.

It was so different seeing young people run after God. And I wanted to catch up. I wanted to have the same zeal and fire that they had; so, I made sure that I always stayed close. Monday I was at leadership training, Tuesday I was at campus fellowship choir rehearsals, Wednesday was mid-week fellowship, and Sunday was church service.

To be at church or involved in church activities was my new normal and I loved it. There was no time for me to go back to the clubs. I only had room for my studies and God.

But as time progressed, I managed to make room for one more priority. It wasn't planned neither was it expected.

His name, *Joseph*.

Joseph was not the typical guy that I thought I would go for. He was different, but in a good way. His love for people and God was what caught my attention. But I would eventually find out that his sense of humour and his ability to out banter me, would be what kept it.

I remember the first day that I ever saw him. It was Sunday 14th March 2010. I remember the date because it was my third ever Sunday at my new church. Back then, our church services were held in one of the screening rooms of Stratford Picture House in London.

Each Sunday we would get a shuttle bus from Birmingham to London to join the service. This particular Sunday, the bus left the campus later than scheduled. As it was my third week in, I had already grasped the structure of the service. Service would begin with opening prayer followed by praise and worship and then the word. As we pulled out of campus and drove along the motorway to London, all I could think about was how sad I would be if I missed praise and worship.

Praise and worship had always been my favourite part of the service. Ever since I could remember, singing was a part of my life. My mum was not one for listening to music in the house or even as she drove us around as kids. But when she did, I could bet my last penny that it would be some good old church hymns playing on full blast whilst my brothers and I sang our hearts out. My parents loved it when I sang and I as grew older my mum would tell me that as soon as I was old enough, I should join the choir at our family church. Which I did. Every Saturday from the age of 12 to 17, I spent my afternoons at choir rehearsals.

As we finally pulled into the parking bay at the Picture House, I and some of the girls I had met through church hurried out of the bus and made our way up the escalators.

"Praise and Worship hasn't started yet!", Cheryl said

As Sharon and I heard that this, we both gave a sigh of relief as we walked through the double doors into the theatre screen. The usher by the door guided us to our seats and, in an attempt not to draw too much attention to ourselves, we quietly shuffled along the row and took our seats.

My association of being a former member of the choir back home meant that anytime I came across a fellow singer, or watched a choir sing at church, I would analyse every member, every harmony and every song choice.

By week two I was able to recognise some of the faces I had seen the previous week. All of the people who sang on my first ever Sunday sang again. However, on week 3, I noticed a new addition to the tenor Section. He was tall, dark and I dare to say, handsome.

He had a smile so big that it filled up the room and as he sang, he used every part of his body to express each word that came out of his mouth.

I stared so hard at him that I wondered if he could feel me watching. I quickly snapped out of it before one of my friends noticed and subjected me to endless ridicule for weeks to come.

***

It was now the end of the service. Typically, after the closing congregational song, we would network with one another until it was time for us to make our way to the shuttle bus and head back to Birmingham. I was hoping that if I rightly positioned myself, Joseph would notice me and say hello. So, I made my way to the aisle closest to the door only a few rows to where he was standing. I convinced Cheryl and Sharon to follow me so we could say hi to some of the people we met the week before. As we all stood and spoke to one another, I could see Joseph from the corner of my eye speaking with what seemed like a multitude of people. It was like people were waiting to speak with him.

'So, he is popular', I thought to myself.

Half an hour had passed, and Joseph hadn't noticed me. Eventually it was time for us to head to the bus, so I got my bag and made my way to the exit.

Throughout the week, I looked forward to church on Sunday but for all the wrong reasons. I couldn't tell if I had a crush on Joseph or if I just wanted his attention. I spent the week planning what I would wear to church that Sunday and how I would do my hair.

The night before church, I opened my closet and began to look for an outfit.

The weather had picked up slightly, so I narrowed down the search to either a skirt or a dress and a cute top or blazer to go with it. After trying on several outfits, I finally landed on a black midi skirt, a white top and a grey blazer. Content with my outfit choice,

I straightened my hair and wrapped it with a scarf so it would be nice and flat for church the following day.

I woke up the next morning extra early so that I could leave enough time to do my makeup. As I walked to the church bus, I tried so hard to pace myself so that I would not sweat out my freshly straightened natural hair.

We arrived at church and it was amazing as always. I noticed from my seat that Joseph was in service. I tried my hardest not to get distracted through the sermon. But I did.

Service was over and it was time for us to mingle with other members. As myself, Cheryl and Sharon left our seats to head toward the back of the screening room, we were stopped by a soothing and gentle voice saying

"Hi ladies, do you guys go to Birmingham?" Turning around, we were met face to face with Joseph.

"Yes, we do." Cheryl replied.

Beside him was another member of the choir. She was average height and slender in stature. I couldn't help wondering if maybe she was his girlfriend.

With a pretty smile plastered on her face, she said, "Nice blazer."

Silence surrounded us, until I realised that she must have been speaking to me as I was the only one wearing a blazer.

"Oh, thank you. It is from River Island' I replied sheepishly.

Joseph introduced himself to us. As he spoke, the smell of his cologne stained the air around us, it was as captivating as the softness of his voice. We stood there for about 5 minutes speaking before our conversation was eventually cut short by one of the many people waiting to speak with him.

We said our goodbyes and we left.

All the way home, I wondered what it was about him that made people gravitate to him. Was it his big puppy dog eyes? Or maybe it was his slight lisp every time he said a word with the letter S.

Week in and week out Joseph and I would exchange a few words after service, until eventually the novelty of my church crush wore off.

SCENE TWO:
SUMMER 2010

First year of university was officially over. A few of my friends stayed in Birmingham to work but I managed to secure a summer job in London, so I went back home. While at home, I signed up to vocal training that one of the leaders at church had started every week. Each week on a Monday evening I would leave work and make my way to East London for the session.

Like every Monday, I made my way to the station and got on the underground to Bow station. But this particular day was different. Today was solo day.

There were four of us that regularly attended the vocal training. For weeks I and the others in the group sessions had been working on individual solos that we would eventually perform in front of the class and a panel of judges. Our instructor wanted to check our progress since we stated.

For weeks we asked our instructor who would be on the panel. And for weeks he kept us guessing. Finally, the week before the session, he eventually gave us a clue.

"He can sing." he said.

"Can we narrow it down any further?" We asked

"He is a part of the church choir and we are good friends."

This narrowed it down to one person; Joseph.

I remember the first time I heard him sing. My jaw literally dropped. His vocal riffs and his ability to make a song his own were second to none.

As I got off the tube at Bow station and walked up the stairs, I felt my palms become wet. I became increasingly consumed by the desire to impress him. Walking into that room felt like I was about to audition for my future.

I was one of the first people to arrive that day. I sat down on one of the empty chairs and prayed in my head that I would not mess this up, eventually everyone began piling in.

As Joseph and the Vocal Trainer took their seats, they opened up with prayer, set out the agenda for the day and gave us a singing order. I looked down at the order set and saw I was singing last. The pressure! I thought to myself. What if everyone is so good and my performance is like the terrible ending of a good movie.

As each person ahead of me sang, I paid great attention to the feedback Joseph gave to them. Everything from how they performed to how he felt listening. I wanted to get it right.

A few vocal warmups and mental prep talks later, it was my turn. I could feel the sweat on my palms and the lump in my throat begin to form.

There is no time for this Sarah, I told myself.

As I stood up and walked to take my place in front of the panel, I introduced myself with a smile. I didn't want to catch his eye, but I certainly wanted my voice to.

The gentle keys of the piano echoed through the air. I waited. Focused on getting it right. Focused on being perfect. I waited. I missed it.

I almost screamed but I doubt that was the sound they expected to hear from me. I kicked myself inside, *how could I miss this moment?*

As I beat myself up inside, hundreds of thoughts ran through my mind. I wondered what he was thinking, how did I look right now? As questions and thoughts buzzed through my mind, and I stood startled, my thoughts were interrupted by a voice.

"Sarah, are you ok? Do you want to try again?" It was my vocal training leader. I looked up in embarrassment, still trying desperately not to catch Joseph's eye.

"Oh, sorry," I said. "Yes please."

Ok, so this is it; take 2. Any more takes Sarah and you may as well take yourself all the way home.

Again, the gentle symphony of the piano pierced the silence in the ear as the introduction to the song began. This time, I counted myself in to avoid a repetition of take 1. I turned my face away from the judges; but I could feel Joseph's gaze piercing through me.

It was almost my cue to come in. I closed my eyes, in an attempt to focus, took a deep breath and I began to sing.

I made sure I sang my heart out that day. Every word came from my soul and every note was carefully articulated to form the most beautiful melody. Until I finished singing, I didn't open my eyes. I couldn't. Finally, I finished singing. Silence echoed through the room; it was deafening. My eyes flew open and darted around the room.

There was something different about this day; I knew it. I had never heard myself sing with such conviction. Amazed and intimidated by my own self, I didn't know what to do. I looked around the room, but I only saw one face; only one stood out. Joseph's.

Across the room I could see him smirking. In his smirk was approval and interest. I didn't need words, I didn't need funny feelings in my stomach, I didn't need my friends to tell me; his face said it all! He was impressed. I could tell by his initial reaction that he was not expecting me to be as good as I was. Heck, I wasn't even expecting it!

I tried to play down my excitement by graciously looking down after completing my solo and avoiding eye contact. I couldn't quite figure out why I wanted to impress him so much. But I was so happy that I did.

When I eventually looked up, I could not hide the huge grin that stretched across my face as Joseph began to positively critique me. As he spoke, my excitement was so loud it drowned out every other sound around me; including Joseph's voice. I could see his lips moving I can just about remember what he said. I walked back to my seat with pride. Anyone would have thought that I had just been nominated for 'Best Female Artist of The Year' at the Grammy's.

The novelty of my church crush hadn't worn off. It was still there. Little did I know that I had just impressed a man that would soon become my first true love.

***

Weeks had passed after the performance at vocal training.

At this point I only saw him as a friend. But the more we spoke and the more I saw him, the more I realised that my feelings for him were no longer platonic. I looked forward to seeing him more than I should, and I found myself in awe every time he came to speak with me.

I battled with what I should do. Do I tell him how I feel and run the risk of him telling me he did not feel the same? I mean since when did a nineteen year old girl from South West London shoot her shot?

As time passed and my feelings were evidently growing, I doubted myself more and more. We had been friends for months now and he has said nothing. Zilch. NADA!

I like to think I am good at reading rooms. And I read this room and I could confidently confirm he didn't feel the same way. After all, I was just the new girl at church trying to find her feet. For all I know, the relationship I had with him was exactly the same as the relationship he had with every other person. I had no business having feelings for him.

Despite me telling myself that I wasn't the kind of girl he would like, my feelings kept growing. As I got closer to a few more people at church, I started to do some undercover investigation work. One of the guys I had recently become friends with was good friends with Joseph. His name was Tolu. Tolu was extremely chatty and was always asking about one girl from my university or another. So, one day I asked Tolu about Joseph. I didn't want to make it obvious that I liked him, so I disguised my motive by throwing in a number of other guys too.

Of course, the main question was is he single! And to my pleasant surprise, the answer was yes. After a while, I wondered if maybe my initial prognosis of the situation was accurate. Maybe I have read the room wrong. Joseph and I went from texting here and there to daily phone conversations that would last hours on end.

I used to love the sound of his gentle voice. Nothing like my loud voice, that's for sure. He was always so eloquent and had a subtle Nigerian accent. I used to call it the international student accent. I never knew that his accent would make this church girl weak.

Okay, that is it!

I decided I was convinced he felt the same way too!

Right?

But if he does, why isn't he saying anything? What kind of man has feelings for a girl and says nothing?

Maybe it is a Christian man thing, I thought to myself.

After all, I had never been with a real Christian man before. Maybe he was taking time to pray about it. Or maybe he didn't want to ruin the beautiful friendship that we had built over the last few weeks.

I toiled for weeks on what to do.

Do I tell him and potentially have what would be the best relationship of all time? Do I not say a word and watch another girl take the man that I want? Or do I tell him and risk ruining everything?

The risk of doing what I really wanted was so high, but eventually, I knew it was a risk that I wanted to take.

Putting my South London pride to the side, I planned out how I would eventually tell him that I liked him. He was planning to visit a few of us at my university that week. On one of the activities I had set out for us to do, I would tell him then.

On the first night of him arriving to my university, I went to visit him at a mutual friend's house where he was staying. I sat on the sofa while he sat on the armchair across the room. In that moment I felt like I could no longer hold it in. I tried so hard. I thought of every conversational topic but somehow this feeling would not go away. I could feel myself exploding on the inside. Before I knew it, I said the words that I would soon learn every man hates to hear.

"We need to talk."

I could feel his heart and mine racing.

Blankly, I looked him in his eyes, and I froze. I knew the words to say but my mouth seized to move. He kept staring at me, waiting for me to speak. But it wasn't coming out.

I immediately regretted opening my 'over-keen-church-boy-smitten' big mouth.

But there was no backing out now.

So, I ran.

Literally!

I got up out of my seat, ran to one of the rooms in the house, closed the door and shouted:

"Please don't follow me!"

Knowing that he would not let this slide, I did what only a

Generation Y child would do; I sent him a text message. Now if this isn't a 21st century love story then I do not know what is.

I text him because the thought of looking at those big eyes and telling him to his face seemed impossible. I wasn't brave enough for the possibilities of what could come out of this conversation.

So, I began to hit the keyboard and text him how I felt about him. I didn't include what that would mean for us. I just simply let him know that I had feelings for him. As soon as I heard the text message alert come through on his phone, I began to panic. What had I just done?

I immediately jumped out of my seat, ran out of the room and slammed the door behind me.

In the 7 seconds it took to get from the room to the communal area, the thought of him rejecting me replayed over and over again. I couldn't risk losing him as a friend but more so, I didn't think my heart could take him rejecting me. So as quickly as I ran out of the room, I ran back into the room and shouted out: *'I know I like you, but I don't want to be with you'*.

I didn't give him the chance to tell me if he felt the same way or the chance to let him speak. Before I could run back out of the room, he asked me to sit down. I thought that maybe, just *maybe*, he would tell me to stop being so silly because he felt the same way too. But the words that echoed from his mouth were the very words I was afraid he would say. "We are better off as friends."

If only I had listened to my friend when she told me to pray first. Maybe God would have saved me from this humiliation. It was painful and embarrassing. I was afraid that this would open up the door to feelings of rejection so, as soon as I got home that evening, I prayed that God would help me to feel better.

The next few weeks were awkward to say the least. We tried to act like everything was normal. I even started dating someone from church. I know. Messy, right?

That didn't last long. He was a nice guy and we got on, but he wasn't Joseph and I didn't have the heart to continue dating him all the while knowing my heart was not ready to move on. After a while, I told myself that I had to get over him. So, I did my best to move on and it was working.

14

SCENE THREE:
READY FOR TAKE OFF

Two months from my awkward conversation with Joseph, news began to spread that he was thinking of relocating back to Nigeria. Upon hearing that I did all I could to try and pick up our friendship before he took his leave. At this point we were seeing each other almost 3-4 times a week. I was a part of a musical production that he wrote so there was no time for awkwardness. Things went back to how it was prior to Sarah's Great and Embarrassing Confession.

In the lead up to the performance, I was Joseph's right-hand man. I was the person he called when he wanted to change something in the play, the person he complained to when someone missed rehearsals and the person he laughed with whenever something humorous happened during practice. We were closer than ever. At first it was hard, but eventually I was okay with being that person to him.

When performance day came, I noticed Joseph was a little bit distant. I put that down to nerves. I tried to speak to him, but his mind was occupied. Pulling him aside, I offered him some encouragement, ensuring him that everything would be great. I knew how much work he put into this play; his vision was finally coming to reality. I was so happy that I could be a part of such a great moment in his life. More than ever, I was happy that we could still be friends. After I said all I had to say I gave him a hug and we got ready for the opening night.

The performance was great. Months of rehearsal and just like that, it was over. There was a great buzz in the air. The cast gathered together in excitement, but I noticed Joseph was missing. I turned to the front of the room and saw him right by the stage. He was removing the microphones from the cables and putting them back in the box. I walked over to give him a hand. Kneeling down to assist him get everything together, without looking directly at me, he told me he felt the same way too. Startled by his statement, I looked up at him.

It had been over three months since I told him how I felt, and this was the last thing I expected to hear. The first two months were so awkward that we barely spoke and the last month we were so occupied with the play that all feelings were put on hold.

I was trying to catch his eye as he spoke. Surely this was a prank. I mean the guy has a sense of humour. But would he really tell me this now? Right after a magical production and only a few weeks before he was relocating back to Nigeria. But the more he spoke, the more I realised that this was not a joke. The vulnerability in his voice, was something I had never heard from him before. I couldn't catch his eye but as he spoke, he caught my heart. Cheesy right?! Yup it was like a double dosage of cheddar in that room because in that instance, with a room full of people, he was the only person I could see.

He told me not to speak. He wanted me to go home and think about what he had said and get back to me.

That was so Joseph. He thought everything out. He wasn't impulsive like how I can be. He knew the risk of what him going back to Nigeria could do to our relationship.

I went home that evening feeling on top of the world.

I was right! He felt the same way too.

I knew when I was on that stage that I wanted us to be together. I went home slept on it and the next day I called him and said I am all in.

***

Our first date was like a fairy-tale.

We planned a romantic evening in London.

Joseph and I loved the theatre. It was one of the many things he and I had in common. We went to watch a production that had been on both of our wish list for months, Wicked.

We arrived at Victoria station about an hour before the play was to begin. I got the train in from Birmingham while he got the underground in from East London where he was staying.

When I arrived, Joseph was already at the station. He welcomed me with a hug before eventually we made our way to the coffee shop next door.

Ever the gentleman, Joseph ordered us some drinks and we sat down. 10 minutes into the coffee, he looked up and announced, "I have a gift for you." I watched as he pulled out a long suede box from his jacket pocket and placed it in my hand.

No man had ever bought me a gift before. Not for my birthday or Christmas. And here he was, on our first date, presenting me a gift for no reason other than to put a smile on my face. Here he was, changing the game. Raising the standard.

Grinning from ear to ear, I opened the box. Inside was a silver bracelet resting on the suede cushion, shinning as the light reflected off it. As he lifted my hands and placed the bracelet on my wrist, I felt like the luckiest girl in the world. I studied the beautiful silver and felt my heart explode. From this day, I wore the bracelet every day.

As Wicked took place on the stage in front of us, my mind was occupied with thoughts of this new 'us': me and Joseph. In his presence I was both excited and nervous. I was a big kid. He brought out a side to me I was unfamiliar with.

As the production unfolded on the stage before us, and my thoughts were preoccupied with this new 'us', from the corner of my eye, I could see Joseph staring at me. I chose to feign ignorance, like I could not feel his large dark eyes burning into my skin.

Gently, he placed his hands in mine and held it throughout the play. Here came the butterflies again, exploding in my stomach. On stage Elphaba began to sing about defying gravity and she was right: something had changed, something wasn't the same… I felt like I was defying gravity.

I looked at our brown fingers interlocked between each other's. there was something comforting about it. I relaxed; slowly, I let down my guard. Next to him, I felt safe.

The night ended and he walked me to my platform and waited with me for my train to arrive. He was the perfect gentleman. My perfect gentleman.

***

My relationship with Joseph was my first experience of a 'church relationship'. I soon learnt that my idea of a church relationship and my reality were two different things. Coming into this, I expected that this would be different to any other relationship I had been in. For starters, Joseph was a Christian and not just by title, but by action and heart. I never had to have the conversation with him that I have chosen to abstain from sex before marriage because quite frankly, this was an expected norm. The perimeters around kissing and touching was something I was not too clear about, but I gathered that we would figure this out along the way.

In a Christian relationship, it was not just a bit of fun; we were together with intention, we had a goal and that goal was compatibility for marriage. We were not dating, we were courting. And all this was new for me.

When I entered into my relationship with Joseph, this was clear in my mind. However, my reality did not just consist of abstinence from sex and intention, it also came with the unsolicited commentary of our peers.

I had never experienced or even witnessed a relationship so scrutinised by an organisation of people. On the one hand, I found it endearing that people cared enough to want to know about our relationship; on the other hand, I found it invasive and intimidating. A church relationship that was widely accepted would have the cheers of many but, for the ones that consisted of an established eligible bachelor and a young lady from South London, barely 9 months in the church, received more stares than cheers.

Joseph was the kind of suitor that any parent would want their daughter to bring home.

He was a leader at the church, he had graduated university with a first class degree and he was respectable. But Joseph was not the only eligible suitor in this relationship. Without blowing my own trumpet, your girl had it going on. I was in my second year at a top 30 university, I loved God and when it comes to looks, I have had no complaints in that department.

In an ideal world, we would be the perfect couple. But in a world where some people still mixed up my name, and in some cases, pretended they couldn't see me, I never made the cut.

Don't get me wrong, the majority of people at my church were great. But amongst Joseph's circle of friends, the pressure to meet the standard of being his girlfriend was one that I never thought I could live up to. On face value, everything seemed fine. But internally, it was a different story. I mean the guy had fans for goodness sake! I just about managed to squeeze in a hug on a Sunday after service if I was lucky.

It was not long before the comments began to roll in. *'Oh she isn't Christian enough' 'Oh he is too good for her'* and the worst, *'he would be better off with his ex'.* It was funny how I was this bubbly and confident person on the exterior yet inside I battled with these insecurities directed to me by people who knew absolutely nothing about me.

This silent battle had such an effect on me, that I considered giving up on us. The court of public opinion had me questioning if I was good enough. I began to believe that I couldn't match up to the standard the crowd had set. I couldn't be this golden, all singing, long skirt wearing, minimal makeup, modest weave wearing woman that they wanted me to be. I mean, I love me some bundles of that Brazilian hair and I am definitely not shy of showing a bit of knee. So, what on earth was I doing here? For the first time in my adult life, I didn't have confidence in myself that I was enough.

To prove to everyone that he had not made a mistake in choosing me, I did all that I could do to win them over. If that meant going to church more or staying at service that bit longer, I would. I made it my business to speak to his 'fans', even those who didn't like me. I did not think there was anything wrong with my dressing, but from that day onwards I chose my wardrobe with every critical voice in mind.

I was miserable.

After what felt like the longest 2 weeks of animated Sarah, I gave up. I stopped trying to be who they wanted me to be and reverted to being the outspoken, confident person that I was. My attempt to be someone else didn't just make me insecure in myself, but also in my relationship.

I never told Joseph how I was feeling. I didn't want him to think I couldn't take the pressure of being his woman. When it was just the two of us, we were fine. But we were so involved in church that we spent a lot of our time around the people I knew did not like me. I was afraid that Joseph's loyalty to these people he had known for years would make him choose them over me. So, I bottled my feelings up hoping that one day it would not bother me.

Like any observant boyfriend, Joseph noticed a change in me. Every time he mentioned my countenance I would act as if I didn't know what he was referring to. I carried this on for a few weeks before I could no longer hold it in.

"It's your people." I said. "They don't know me and they hate me."

I began to tell him all that had been going on. He let me get it out. Feeling after feeling, thought after thought, fear after fear; I told him everything and he listened without interrupting. When I finally let him speak, I was instantly calmed by the gentleness of his voice.

"Sarah, you are the one I want."

And with those 6 words, every insecurity I had felt like they never existed to begin with. Every fear, every anxious thought, every doubt all dissipated at the truth of his words. I had the greatest reassurance that a girl could ask for. I had him. And I wasn't a fan; I was his girl. The one he wanted.

It didn't matter what others said because I was more than enough for him. Publicly he defended my honour and privately he affirmed it. It didn't bother him that I was loud, wore 20-inch Brazilian hair and always had nail extensions. Everything I tried to change about me to fit in all formed a part of the very things that attracted him to me.

What more could I ask for?

He made me feel like the most important person in the world; more importantly, his world. With each day, he reminded me that I was what he wanted. It didn't matter if people thought I was no good for him because to him, I was more than what he could have ever dreamed of. I was the girl he chose. And he was the guy who captured my heart. It didn't take long before I realised that I was falling in love with him.

It was safe to say that Joseph was my best friend. There was not a decision I made that he was not in support of. For every venture, he was my cheerleader and for every tough day, he was my shoulder to cry on. I lost count on the amount of times I would fall asleep and wake up with the phone pressed to my ear; we avoided getting off the phone at all costs. Once I woke up, I would continue the conversation where we left off. Eventually we would hear the tune of the birds whistling as they welcomed the sunrise. That was our cue to say goodbye and get ready for the day ahead.

He was my person.

Like most girls in love, I had already pictured our perfect life together. I had never been so happy.

Only a few weeks after we officially began to date, it was time for Joseph to go to Nigeria.

The news that he may be relocating was true. I knew this day was coming and instead of preparing for what this could mean for us, I spent each day falling more and more in love with him; guarding my heart from my boyfriend was not an option. Little did I know that this would make the next few years of our relationship almost unbearable to navigate.

I was so in love with him that I wanted to make us work. Some of the people at church would ask us how we would make it work. While others were probably hoping that it wouldn't. I was so nervous to tell my friends outside of church that Joseph would be leaving the country. The majority of whom were yet to meet him.

How would I even start the conversation: *"Oh, by the way, you know that guy I have been telling you about? The one who makes me happy, completes all my sentences and gets all my jokes? He is going to be moving to another continent next week and I don't know when I will next see him."*

I hoped that the longer I pretended it was not happening, that it wouldn't happen at all. But I was wrong. Ignorance wasn't really bliss because when you finally acknowledged what you were attempting to avoid, you're met with many ways you could have prepared and handled the situation with wisdom. In the short duration of time that we were together, we had never experienced something that would test our relationship in this way. I had no measure of trial to compare this to. I had to have faith in the unknown and I was afraid.

***

I had an assessment the day Joseph went back to Nigeria.

My boyfriend was leaving the country and I couldn't even accompany him to the airport.

I spent the morning feeling lost. But deep down inside of me, I knew that we would be okay.

We had a plan. One that we were committed to. We would call each other every day, video call at least 3 times a week, and we'll Blackberry message each other constantly.

The call rates for an international call to Nigeria on T-Mobile was astronomical so I got myself a second phone and a pay as you go sim card with international call bundles. For those of you from an African household and living in the UK, I am sure your mum has sent you to top up her Lyca mobile more times than you can count.

We had a system and we were determined to make it work.

In the first few weeks of our long distance relationship, things were amazing. We spoke as much as we possibly could. I couldn't have been happier. I wondered why I was so nervous in the first place. After all, he was my person and we are meant to be together.

When he arrived to Nigeria, he told everyone about me. His sisters, his parents and all of his friends. He was so proud to call me his girlfriend and I was proud to bear that title. Each day on our calls, I would anticipate just how long it would be before I heard his younger sister, Mena scream "Hi Sarah!" down the phone. It had only been a few weeks and already he was introducing me to his family.

There was not a week that went by that we didn't speak about our future. About how he would spend our marriage spoiling me and I would spend it making him the happiest man alive. In front of me, he had no guard. I knew about the struggles he faced while being back home and I also knew just how much our calls represented the new home he had found in England. Me.

With each day we grew closer and closer. But the closer we got, the more the pain of our distance became unbearable for us both. But mostly him.

We went from speaking multiple times a day to sometimes not speaking at all. Afraid of what this could mean, I voiced my concerns to Joseph before it was too late. He assured me that I had nothing to worry about. I wanted to believe him, so I went against my better judgment and I did. I comforted myself by excusing the lack of communication to him not being able to bear me being so far away.

But how long could I tell myself this? Would it be after the third time he would go days without speaking to me? Or would it be after he would ignore my messages so much that I felt like a telecommunicator sale rep. Things got worse and eventually, I was beginning to notice his countenance towards me changing too. He no longer sounded like the softly spoken man with the gentle tone that I met at Stratford picture house.

His voice had developed a base and increased some decibels; he sounded angry. If rage was a person, it would be him.

I thought maybe if I called him more, instead of messaging all the time, he would answer more. But call after call the phone would ring out with no response. I got so used to hearing *"The MTN line you are calling is not available."* that I contemplated forming a relationship with his service provider instead.

After a while he stopped letting the phone ring to the operator and began declining my calls. My mind was consumed with anxious thoughts. What if he went back to Nigeria and was acquainted with his old life or an old girlfriend? In the time we were together, we never really spoke about his life prior to him moving to England. We were so led by feelings that we never spoke about his past. Or mine. He could have a whole secret life and I would be none the wiser. There was not a conspiracy theory I did not think of and what made it worse was that he stopped being there to address my concerns.

The limited communication we did have was full of arguments. We argued about everything from communication to commitment.

The distance was killing our relationship.

Dear Diary,

It's hard to believe that there once was a time that Joseph and I were head over heels in love.

Now I am here, wondering if I should be running for the hills.

I never thought the day would come that I would question whether Joseph truly loved me.

I knew that choosing to pursue a relationship with him would be challenging. I knew that there was a possibility that the distance would eventually take its toll. But never did I imagine that a long distance relationship with Joseph would form some of the most emotionally distressing years of my life to date.

Every time I think we are better something happens that takes us 3 steps back.

I don't know how much more of this I can handle. When will we be so set back that it is no longer worth us trying to move forward?

Signed,
A scared girlfriend.

SCENE FOUR:
BEGINNING OF THE END

What if him moving back was all it took for him to realise that I was a mistake? That maybe everyone was right; I was not the right girl for him. These were the questions I would ask myself as I dialled Joseph's number, hoping for once he would pick up.

How was it that our relationship was on the verge of collapsing but the love I had for him grew stronger and stronger?

How do I explain the feeling to always want to protect him and his character to those around us even though I knew that the man they knew him to be was not the man he was to me. That the affectionate man they all loved did not have enough affection left to tell me he loved me.

I knew that by staying in this relationship I was setting myself up for a future that consisted of misery and pain. But the thought of leaving him was one that I could not handle.

So instead of walking, I began looking for answers and, in some respects, I began to excuse his behaviour. I blamed the change in our relationship on the state of his emotions. He was extremely unhappy when he moved back to Nigeria. For months he tried to get a job in the UK to satisfy the conditions of his postgraduate work visa but it was to no avail. Nigeria may have been his home, but he wasn't ready to go back when he did.

Rather than acknowledging the signs that he was unwilling to let me in, I tried to force my way in. And I failed. I never understood why women tried to fix a man until I became that woman. I was too busy playing 'Bob the Builder' that I couldn't see I didn't have the tools to fix him. And the more I tried and failed, the more rejected I felt.

Embedded in the fibre of this loving man was a man bitter about life. A man who didn't think he deserved happiness. Yet there I was, second guessing myself, believing the lie that I wasn't enough.

And so instead of counting my losses and leaving, I saw this as a direct challenge to do all I could to remind him that I could make him happy. I was the same girl that he chose even when so many told him not to. The one who he would call and speak to until the birds started singing. The one who made him smile after every rough day.

Initially, I wanted him to be happy because his unhappiness made me unhappy. But if I am honest, after a while I tried so hard to make him happy because I believed if he was happy then maybe he would love me better. But this was not the case. The harder I tried, the more I failed. Joseph taught me first-hand that an unhappy man in singlehood will not automatically become happy when he gets into a relationship.

The unhappiness he was experiencing was something only God could turn around. And every moment I tried to make him happy in my own strength, he only drifted further and further away.

Before long we were the classic case of dysfunction. One month we were on and the next we were off. On his trip to the UK, he was the perfect boyfriend and on my trips to Lagos, I was his perfect girlfriend. But whenever we were apart, we would go back into the cycle of endless arguments and tear-filled nights. Joseph was my first true love and I wanted to do anything I could to fight for our relationship.

For starters, I didn't want the naysayers to have one over on me. I mean, can you imagine their faces if we had broken up? The *'I told you sos'*. In hindsight I recognise it was such a terrible and irresponsible reason to stay committed to a relationship. But can I be real; that was an additional burn that I did not want to take. But more than my pride being bruised, I didn't want to lose the friendship we once had. I knew crossing the line from friend to boyfriend was a risk and one I took because somewhere in my nineteen-year-old heart, I believed he was the one.

But the man I was with now was no longer the friend I once knew. It became harder to excuse the state of our relationship. On numerous occasions we would fight, block each other on social media and then make up again. For two years, this was our normal.

We were on and off and then on and then off again. And before I knew it, it had been over a year since we were last on.

SCENE FIVE:
THE BREAKUP

After a while it became too hard to keep trying. Eventually he told me that he thought it was best I let him go. I was distraught. I tried so hard to make us work. I held on to the man I knew instead of facing the man right in front of me. After we broke up, I was heartbroken. I promised myself that I would never allow him, or any other guy, to make me feel so broken again.

When we called it quits, I was so determined to forget about him. I deleted him off my blackberry messenger, unfollowed him from Facebook and blocked him from twitter. I was guarding my heart. But what use is guarding your heart when at every given opportunity, I would use my housemates phone to stalk his Facebook and twitter feed and, on the odd occasion, ask her to put up a hot picture of me as her BBM (Blackberry Messenger) display picture so he knew exactly what he was missing.

We were supposed to be a *Christian couple*; and they aren't supposed to breakup. But the truth is, there is no such thing as an unbreakable relationship. And this idea I had of a Christian couple being a perfect couple centred on God alone and absent of flaws was a myth. I put so much into fulfilling what I thought was the picture perfect Christian couple that I failed to see that we were two Christian human beings in a relationship.

Our faith was there to hold a mirror to the issues we didn't know we had and for that I will forever be grateful. But this idea that my faith would make me exempt from these issues was one of the reasons why I was upset with God when we broke up. I wanted to know why God would let me stay in this relationship for 2 years only for it to crumble. But our faith doesn't excuse our inadequacies, It simply gives us the grace and the tools to get through them. This realisation helped me to see that God wasn't to blame for my decisions, I was.

I didn't know how to be single anymore. I was so use to my life being intertwined with Joseph's, like our fingers were on our first date in the theatre. I knew that in order for me to fully move on, I couldn't look back. I tried to fill my time with things. I got my driving licence, graduated from university, enrolled onto my masters and started a new job. My life was busy. But my heart was still stuck. I had to shift my focus away from trying to distract myself from missing Joseph and shift it towards healing.

This new season of singleness was an opportunity for growth, it was not a death sentence as I had subconsciously ascribed it to be. It allowed me to work through some of my issues without carrying the weight of someone else's. I spent my year of singleness thriving. This meant no more attention seeking antics from Joseph, no getting into a new relationship and a whole lot of trusting God that He knew what is best for me.

I resubmit my heart to God so that He could heal every broken piece of it. I was 22, lost a whole lot of weight and every day, I was healing.

SCENE SIX:
HEATWAVE

Summer 2013 was a summer to remember. I was down 40lbs, single and loving it. After the back and forth with Joseph and I, I made sure that I enjoyed the summer break to the fullest.

The weather that year had been more favourable to us than the typical London summers that consisted of 2 weeks of sunshine and 2 months of rain. It was only right that I took full advantage of being single, trimmed and tanned; so, I made sure to be at every motive worth going to.

It was a Saturday afternoon and me and my friend, Annabel were on our way to Lola's family BBQ. I was driving while Annabel was the designated DJ in the passenger seat. As she skipped through the tracks to select the next song, a call came through.

"You've got a call coming through from a +234 number, babes."

"234?" I scowled. "That's a Nigerian area code. Which one of my family members is calling me now? If it is important, they will call back."

We let the phone go to voicemail and once the ringing stopped, Annabel pumped up the music and I continued to drive. Shortly after we pulled up to a local supermarket and Annabel popped in to pick up some drinks for the BBQ.

A few minutes after Annabel left the car, the same +234

number called again. Worry that the call may be urgent from a cousin or an auntie, prompted me to answer the call.

"Hello...hello?" I said again, waiting for someone to answer. Silence came through. I couldn't tell if it was a bad line or if the person on the other end was simply refusing to speak.

"If you can hear me, I can't hear you." Just as I was ready to hang up the phone, the person on the other end finally spoke.

"Hello Sarah." I froze. My heart dropped into my stomach. Everything stood still. *"It's Joseph."*

*"*I know who this is," I said with a slight sense of confusion in my voice. I knew it was him the moment he said hello. The moment his voice travelled through the line from Nigeria to London, I time travelled back to the summer we met; the first time I saw his dark skin stand out amongst everyone else. His voice captured my attention like that first time I saw him on that Sunday morning. There was always something about the way he said my name that commanded my attention. After all of our time apart, it took a couple of words for him to take me back to a place I had spent a year overcoming.

"Excuse the shock, but I didn't expect to hear from you." I paused. "Is everything ok?" I asked.

*"*I am good. Work is amazing and family are good. I just thought I would tell you that I got accepted onto my Masters. I'll be moving to the North of England in September."

Hearing this news caught me completely off guard. I didn't know what to say or how to react. On the one hand, my heart was filled with glee. While we were together, I prayed non-stop that he would come back to England. God was finally answering my prayers. But on the other hand, I was confused. What did this mean? I spent the last year of my life working on being a better me. I couldn't risk going back to that miserable girl he left.

As I began getting lost in my thoughts, I saw Annabel walking back towards the car with bags in her hands. I didn't want her to know that Joseph called me. I needed to find a way to end the call before she got back to the car. Seeing her approaching closer to the car door, I snapped out of my reverie and responded to Joseph.

"Joseph, I am so sorry, I've got to go. But I will call you back." Annabel opened the car door just as I hit the call end call button. She got in the car and I drove off like nothing happened.

As we made our way to the BBQ, all I could think about was

the unexpected phone call and abrupt conversation. I tried to unpack my feelings, but I couldn't make out how I really felt about him moving back. And that scared me.

After the BBQ ended, I dropped Annabel home and stopped over at an off licence store to pick up an international calling card. I spent the whole time at the BBQ feeling bad at how abruptly I ended the call. He had called to share good news with me. I could have at least said congratulations. I didn't want to wait till I got home to call him back, so I sat in my car and entered in the details from the calling card. The phone barely rang when Joseph picked up. He must have known it was me.

"I didn't think you would call me back." Joseph said in his usual cheeky tone.

And of course, I had to be cheeky right back, "Neither did I." I said proudly, as I smiled through the phone. "So, your Masters… look at you following in my footsteps." I teased.

"They are great steps to follow."

"Agreed." We both laughed and it felt good.

We barely spoke about his move to the UK in that call. Instead we spent the time catching up and comparing notes on the latest season of Grey's Anatomy. Like the old days, we continued to banter until the credit on the call card eventually ran out.

But I would soon hear back from him. The next day Joseph called me. And the day after that and the day after that. Between the time he called me on the way to the BBQ and the day he landed in the UK, Joseph and I spoke every day.

I woke up each day looking forward to speaking with him. The excitement of coming back to England gave him a new lease of life. He sounded like his old self. He had something to look forward to and I could tell that he was happy.

The more we spoke, the clearer it was to me that Joseph still had feelings for me. But he was not the only one that still had feelings. I did too. I missed his friendship so much when we broke up and now I had it again. I didn't want to risk losing it. So I made a decision to not give in. We could flirt all we wanted but I had to be strong.

***

Over the last month and a half, I tried to come to terms with the fact that he was going to be in the same country as me. He would be in up North while I was living in London.

I told myself that we would barely see each other which lowered the chances of me and him getting emotional involved. I convinced myself that he could be close enough to maintain a friendship but far enough for us to keep our relationship platonic. I was determined for us not to ruin what we had built over the last few weeks.

Just as I came to terms with his relocation, things changed. Joseph had turned down the offer at the university in the up north and accepted an offer at a London university.

This was going to be harder than I thought.

I knew him moving to London would mean he would likely come back to the same church and we would be a part of the same circles. Several of the people who were against our relationship had now moved on to other churches so that did not worry me. What worried me was the frequency of us seeing each other. There was no way I could see him every Sunday and at social events without my feelings growing stronger. But was this really a bad thing? Maybe this is all a part of God's plan for us?

Honestly, I was confused.

Now I knew that he would be moving to London, I wanted him to know that I had grown in God since the last time we were together and so I made sure that I invited him to the church's annual conference which happened to fall in the week of his return.

He accepted the invite to conference. This was going to be the first time I saw him in over a year. I had to make sure I looked cute enough for him to see how good I looked but covered enough for him to know that I am still saved; balance.

After finding the perfect outfit, all that was left for me to do was to practice my reaction for when I saw him. I wanted a balance between excited and unbothered, calm and cool, old-Sarah-you-fell-in-love-with, and new-Sarah-who's-grown-but-you-can-fall-in-love-with-again; balance.

Standing in front of that mirror reciting different ways of saying *'oh my gosh, it's great to see you'* took me back to the days where I would long for Sunday services just so my heart can be warmed by the sight of his smile.

Joseph was back in town and it only took one glance at him for me to know that I wanted us to try again. I tried to ignore these feelings. But it was so hard to. I had multiple voices in my ear from some of our biggest cheerleaders who appeared to be more excited about his return back to London than I was! They took his return as a sign that we were meant to be.

On the flip side I had a few people who were out right against us getting back together. They had seen me cry through the pain of our previous break up and my happiness was far too important to them to watch me get hurt again. I tried my hardest not to be swayed by either voice and just follow my intuition.

But then I saw him, it was game over. He looked good, his cologne still made my knees quiver and I wanted him to be mine.

Up until now, I hadn't told him how I felt. I am sure he could tell but I was insistent on not letting anything get in the way of me doing the right thing. I prayed and prayed but I heard nothing from God. To be honest, my heart knew what it wanted, and it wanted him and at the same time, my mind couldn't ignore the red flags of the past that I feared would creep into our future. There was this constant battle of what the heart wanted and what my mind wanted. So, the truth was, even if God was speaking to me, I was not sure if I could hear it.

All my adult life all I wanted in a man was for him to love me, know me and care for me. I saw the fairy-tale standard of a Hollywood relationship but never in real life. I grew up watching the dysfunction from the relationships around me and I knew that I wanted better for myself. I wanted someone who would see my pain even when I had a smile plastered on my face. Someone who would uplift me not only with his words but with prayers. I wanted a man who knew me.

So when I had a dream a few days later, I knew that God had heard me. In the dream, I was broken on the inside but smiling to the world. Joseph walked into the room I was in, turns to my close friend and asked, "What's wrong with Sarah?" This friend, in particular, always knew when I was upset, but in the dream, she said "Nothing, she is fine." A few moments later, Joseph approached me, tenderly kissed my forehead and whispered, "I am here." He stood right beside me. He could see what others could not and he loved me in a way I had not seen in my own life. That dream to me was a sign from God that I would not have to look for his love the way I once did.

I never told Joseph about the dream. I waited for him to make the first move.

Sometime had passed since he had moved back, and he hadn't said anything. Okay let me be honest, it had only been two days but when it came to him, I was all of a sudden impatient. And who could really blame me. A few days ago, he was serenading me with romantic and flirtatious messages.

This time around, I wasn't that overly brave, finger happy, feeling telling, expose herself to the guy she likes, nineteen year old. I was older and a lot smarter. This was not the time for me to 'shoot my shot'. So instead of running along and telling him how I felt, I did what any girl in my position would do, I waited, and I made sure I looked damn good while doing so.

I showed off my new figure and made sure those bundles he liked were tight and intact. My nails were his favourite nail colour and my dimples were on permanent display

Evidently, waiting worked. A few days later, he asked me out for coffee, and we sat in a coffee shop for hours and laughed and reminisced on the days when we enjoyed each other's company. By the end of our 3-hour coffee meeting, he asked to take me out for dinner. Of course I had to act a little hard to get and check my diary (which by the way, I knew was clear) eventually after seeing how I could 'fit him in'. I responded, "is Tuesday good for you?"

It was Tuesday morning. I struggled to sleep through the night. I didn't know what to expect. I got ready for work that morning anticipating what was to come later that evening. As excited as I was at the prospects of Joseph being back in my life, I couldn't help but think about all of the reservations I once had, the reservations I still had. Don't get me wrong, coffee was great. I felt as special as I did when we first got together. Three years had passed, and he still gave me butterflies. But were butterflies enough? I was so confused, but I knew that we were both different, so I was willing.

The day of our dinner I sat at work thinking about our date later in the evening. Was it even a date or was I just over thinking it? As I patiently waited for 5.30 pm to strike, I thought about all of the ways I knew he would make me laugh that evening.

Finally, it was time to leave the office. I met up with him at Oxford Circus and we walked down to a beautiful Italian restaurant. It felt like our first date all over again. Just as I imagined, the dinner was perfect. We laughed, reminisced over a bottle of wine and did what we both love to do; eat. The night was like something out of a fairy-tale. Well almost. Our romantic candle lit dinner for two was followed by a less romantic trip to McDonalds for some McFlurrys. Joseph had a sweet tooth and the bougie desserts in the restaurant was not going to cut it.

As we walked down the street with our ice cream in hand, he asked me to start a journey of forever with him. Calm down, he didn't propose over 99p ice cream. The proposal would come exactly a year later.

But on this day, he promised that this time would be different. There will be transparency all the way and a promise of a better him. He accepted the offer at the London university for me. He changed the course of his life because he believed that I was it for him.

I had never seen him so intentional about what he wanted. And just like that, I looked at his face and saw the guy who sat on the stage. The one who protected me and defended me. I didn't see the times I wish he was there for me, or even the tears he made me cry. I didn't remember how the butterflies he made me feel now, was a feeling that I had felt before. These butterflies that fluttered about happily in my stomach, turned into aches in my stomach when distance separated us. I put these thoughts to the back of my mind and all I saw was the him who made me feel like the luckiest girl in the world.

There were no shortcuts, no 'let's-date-and-see-how-it-goes'; he came in and he came strong. How could I deny that? I was so sure that the broken-hearted girl I was running from would never return. This time was different. We are older now and we were working towards one goal, marriage.

SCENE SEVEN: REUNITED

When we got back together, our friends were happy for us. And as time went on, even those who had doubts began to cheer us on. We became a couple that everyone was rooting for.

My mum was so happy when Joseph and I got back together. She loved him almost as much as she loved me. And of course, it helped that he would feed into her love for bags and randomly purchase her a bag whenever he saw something that he thought would tickle her fancy.

My brothers and my dad were the last to know about Joseph. Growing up as their younger sister and my father's precious daughter meant that no matter how old I was, I was afraid to let them know that I had a boyfriend. Eventually I had to let them know. I was tired of getting dressed up for dates and wearing massive coats out of the front door so they wouldn't ask me where I was going all dressed up.

My brothers surprisingly warmed up to Joseph a lot quicker than I thought. They were all Manchester United supporters so that helped break the ice. Joseph had a way of gravitating to people and it was not long before they formed a beautiful relationship.

My dad on the other hand took a little longer to warm to Joseph. In his eyes I was his baby girl and all of a sudden, this 6ft man was coming to take his princess away. But after a few home visits and telephone calls, Joseph and my dad got on like a house on fire. All the people in my life loved him but more importantly, they loved the way he loved me.

Joseph was my biggest cheerleader. All he was missing was some pom poms and the cute outfit. When I launched my business, he was right there beside me promoting it to everyone who would listen. And if they didn't, he would make them. When I was inundated with deliveries, he would personally do them for me.

Don't get me wrong, like all couples, we had our odd disagreements here and there, but being in the same country and seeing one another regularly meant that unlike before, we could work through them. I could genuinely see that this time was different. I was so much more than a girlfriend to him. I was his safe place. His best friend. His personal person.

In the back of my mind, I wondered how long this would last for. Once Joseph's post graduate degree was over, he would have a three-month window to find a job in London or he will have to move back. I was so overjoyed by Joseph's intentionality when he asked us to try again that I never asked the hard questions before diving into our relationship. His great plan was for him to not have to move back. But what would happen if this plan failed?

One thing was for sure, distance doesn't work for us. And as much as Nigeria was his home, it changed him in a negative way. The thought of him going back and falling into old habits frightened me. I knew I had to trust him, that in the event he did have to go back, that he would be strong enough not to fall back into a cycle of unhappiness followed by leaving church and neglecting his friends. But even if he was strong enough, I didn't know if our relationship was.

Sometimes I thought that we were stronger than ever. Unbreakable. But other times, I wondered if we should have started from scratch. Instead of uprooting our foundation and starting afresh, we began to compile the good and the bad and soon I was afraid that elements of our relationship would begin to sink. We never really dealt with why the distance changed him the way it did. For now, it was okay because there was no distance. But what if somewhere down the line, all of these unresolved issues hit the surface.

We were growing deeper in love and had no clear strategy of what we would do if the only option was for him to move back. I knew that there were still a few months before we had to deal with it. I tried to stay in the present as much as I could but the fear of our future was at the back of my mind.

***

It was coming to the end of the academic year and nothing seemed to be happening with Joseph's job applications. Joseph and I had started to speak about our future and, being the traditional man he was, I knew that him not being able to secure a job while I had already started my career, was grating on him. I knew that Joseph would consider going back to Nigeria, but I hoped that this would be his last option and not his safe one.

It was one month until his official course end date and I could sense that Joseph felt the pressure. I could sense it because I often got the brunt of his mood swings. But with every outburst, he reassured me that we would be ok. That he will keep trying until something came up. I wanted to believe him, so I did.

***

It was a Saturday afternoon after choir practice. My usual routine was to meet up with Joseph for a date night or we would have dinner at one of our houses. This particular Saturday, I went to his.

When I pulled up to the house, Joseph came downstairs to let me in. The familiar aroma of his infamous pasta bake drifted through the air into my nostrils. I loved his pasta bake. It was the one thing he made better than me.

We went into the dining area and he dished me out some food. Once we finished our food, we went upstairs to watch a movie. Halfway through the movie, Joseph paused the film.

"I have something to tell you." He said

Instantly I sat up. His voice was far too serious for my liking. I could tell by the look in his face that this was something that would shake me.

"What is it?" I said.

And that is when he told me the news I was dreading to hear; he decided to move back to Nigeria.

"What do you mean you have decided? Without speaking to me?"

I couldn't believe what was happening. I didn't know what to be more upset about. The fact that he was leaving or that he had

39

made the decision without consulting me. This was the same guy who discussed something as trivial as getting a new pair of shoes with me. Yet for a decision this big, one that would change our lives forever, he had already made up his mind without so much as uttering a word to me.

I felt betrayed. At least last time we were together he already made the decision to leave before he got with me. I was in denial for a few days that this was happening. When it finally hit me, I begged him not to do this to us. His course was ending next month but he still had several months on his visa. The look in his eyes was that of a man who didn't want to go. I thought that maybe, just maybe, there was room for him to change his mind.

I prayed so hard that he would get a job here. I prayed, I fasted, you name it.

When things were not happening at the pace he wanted, I knew that even though he promised me he would stick it out, he would choose the easy option.

SCENE EIGHT:
I DO?

It was the week of our anniversary and he made our anniversary celebrations spread over the course of the week. Initially, I thought it was over the top, but by no means was I surprised. He had always been romantic. He was the man who made all of our male friends look bad because of his lavish gestures.

Each day we did something different together. Something that represented our relationship. We did everything from watching a musical in the West End, going to the arcade like a bunch of teenagers, pancakes in the city, indoor skydiving, a spa weekend and a romantic dinner on a river cruise. But the best day of the 7 days of fun was Friday the 12th September. It was the day he gathered our loved ones together and asked me to be his wife.

I couldn't believe it! Instantly my mind went back to the day of the McFlurry ice cream. The day he promised me that one day, I would be his wife.

The proposal was something out of a movie that I had personally written. Almost everything I could have possibly wanted happened on that day.

With all the time that had passed, with all the pain between the present day and September 12th 2014, I can still remember the way I felt that day.

I remember walking towards the restaurant holding his hand. The closer we got to the door, the more I noticed the tenderness of his palms. I wore a red dress and a pair of new heels that I was yet to break into. I kept slowing down so I could catch my balance. We continued walking and as we took steps towards the entrance, he began to slow down until he eventually stopped walking. I assumed he stopped walking because of me.

"Is everything okay, babe?" I asked.

"Just perfect." He responded with a knowing smile. His gaze gently traced over my face, taking in every part of it, until they landed on my eyes. As he looked me in the eyes, his soft voice hummed like September's gentle breeze over my skin, "I love you."

I drank him in, trying to keep my breathing steady. My stomach was filled with butterflies. All these years on and he still gave me butterflies.

We continued to walk towards the restaurant. As he opened the doors, I heard the sweet serenade of one of my favourite love songs being sang accompanied by the beautiful melody of the piano.

Joseph released his grip on my hand and walked ahead. In that moment, I knew exactly what was happening. And with tears rolling down my face I froze.

Our friends and family stood on either side of the room, creating a perfect gateway for me to walk down the aisle to meet my prince. The red carpet leading up to him was decorated with rose petals and tea light candles. All the emotions of our first valentine's day together came rushing back.

It finally hit me that the voice I could hear singing was one all too familiar. It was the voice of one of my beautiful sisters. I remembered telling him one night as we watched a movie that when we get married, I want our friend, Val to sing me down the aisle. I was amazed that even little details like that was factored into this day. Streams of tears continued to roll down my cheeks. I eventually summoned the courage to keep walking. As I walked, I was met by placards with different messages and quotes that signified our love.

The closer I got to the end, the closer I was to being greeted by my boyfriend down on one knee with a ring in his hand. I was overwhelmed and humbled by the fact that someone could love me this much to make me his wife. That someone could plan every detail of, what would be the beginning of the rest of our lives in such a way, that it would stay with me forever.

How can I forget the ring! Do you know how good it felt to not have to pretend I liked my engagement ring? I mean, I just about sent a picture of my dream ring to all 237 contacts in my phone and this rock in the box exceeded all of my expectations.

As he knelt there, I thought that I was the luckiest woman in the world.

I stood before him and he promised to always be there for me, never leave me, always celebrate me and the list went on. I was blown away by every word that came out of his mouth.

And then it was time. The four-word sentence I had been waiting for our entire relationship and that I imagined the whole of my life.

"Will you marry me?"

I took one glimpse into his eyes and at that heavy piece of bling in the box, and confidently and proudly said, yes.

Life couldn't get any better. I kept pinching myself. I couldn't believe it. I was going to marry the man of my dreams. I was right, it was meant to be, and we were untouchable.

There was not a day that went by that I didn't pray for him to say *babes, I am staying.*

But the vision I hoped for as a response to this prayer was shattered when an opportunity came for Joseph to work at one of the top banks in Nigeria.

I hadn't even known he had been applying for jobs there. But I should have known he would. This was Joseph. The day he got the call offering him the job, everything inside of me wanted to shut down. But the supportive fiancé in me knew that in that moment I had to celebrate the man I loved for landing such a great opportunity.

He turned to me and said "Babes, it is true what the bible says. He who finds a wife truly does find favour."

I laughed and responded, "That's me… Miss Favour."

But deep down inside of me, I was not laughing. I was crying. How can 'favour' be tearing us a part? Surely favour would have been that he found a job here, in England. Heck, I don't even mind if it was in Wales or in Scotland. At least they were train journeys away.

Ten days after he proposed, he moved to Nigeria. And when he did, I resented him.

I was about to get into a marriage with a man I was harbouring resentment for. The feeling of bitterness towards any human being is not productive and instead of growing, you find that you're regressing. But the feeling of bitterness towards your partner brings you to a whole new level of dangerous territory.

Don't get me wrong, I was so happy to be his fiancé, and, in that moment, it was exactly what I thought we needed. But as the days led up to his departure, all I could think was why? Why would he propose to me?

Our proposal was featured on a popular social media wedding page called Bella9ja, Wedding Digest and so much more. In the comments section we were labelled as the 'good looking couple' and it wasn't long before we qualified as #Goals.

Now please don't get me wrong, the whole experience was magical, but magic is for fairy tales. All of those likes and comments couldn't take away the anxiety I felt. I knew he loved me, but did he only ask me to marry him so that I would stay with him when he left? If he didn't go back to Nigeria for work, would he have proposed when he did? These questions are all questions that I harboured until it would eventually eat me up inside. Questions I should have asked my fiancé when I had the chance! But I didn't. And in not doing so, I created my own conclusions and the resentment grew. Resentment I could have avoided if I was less worried about upsetting him and more intentional about starting our future together the right way.

You have to remember this was not going to be the first time we would have tried long distance. The first time failed! Miserably.

Could we really do this? We had gone too far to back out now. But was getting engaged too much too soon? Truthfully, basing our past experience as the main motivator not to try long distance again felt unfair to me. Not because it was not important, but because in the past, he moved away only weeks after we started courting. At least this time we had more time together. But in the course of us re-courting, there were many moments where I questioned if we could survive under pressure. And that is when we were in the same city let alone being in different continents.

The night before he left, he stayed over at mine so I could give him a lift to the airport in the morning. We sat in my kitchen and tried to speak about anything other than the fact that he was leaving the next day. But it wasn't long before my top was drenched in my tears. This was really our last night together. I started to think about how we had wasted the previous week arguing. I was going to miss him so much and all I wanted to do for the rest of that night was lay my head on his chest and hold on so tight that he wouldn't want to let go.

Sure enough, I couldn't sleep at all that night. I got out of bed and got ready for the airport run. The entire journey from my house to the airport was practically in silence with a few comments here and there. I couldn't understand why every other time we drove to Heathrow that early there seemed to be traffic but, on this day, the roads were clear. All I wanted was more time. And, I mean, it wouldn't be that bad if he missed his flight, right?

I was so afraid that anything would set me off and I would start bawling like a baby again. As we pulled into terminal 5, I became more and more anxious; it was actually happening.

We rolled his suitcase through the airport and queued up for check in. The queue was moving a lot faster than I appreciated. Every moment I could savour before he had to go through security was very much welcomed. As we got closer to the front I stood there and thought about all the ways I could get on that plane.

He checked in and we walked towards the security clearance point. "Wait. Let's just stay here for a bit." He said. We stood in front of *Boots* and talked for as long as we could, until it was time for him to go through security.

For the next 19 months of our relationship, we lived apart. And I will be the first to say that the pressures of distance is one of the many reasons why I am writing this memoir.

Over the next few chapters, I will share with you the story of how what I thought was an unbreakable love that was broken through a series of events that was shielded from the public eye.

I am going to take you behind the scenes of the picture perfect.

PART 2

Dear Diary,

It has been 6 months since Joseph left and 6 months since we started planning our wedding. I say 'we', but really it is all me.

Planning this wedding by myself has been lonely. I knew that with Joseph being away the burden would fall mostly on me, but I never expected to be doing this alone.

I know he is thousands of miles away and it would be unreasonable for me to expect him to video call into every vendor meeting or watch me over a screen as I taste the cakes we plan to serve at our wedding.

But is responding to messages really that hard? I have lost count of the amount of times I would message him and receive no response. If I was lucky, I might get a response several hours later. It's like as soon as he sees the word wedding, he doesn't see anything else.

And let's not start with the calls. It is 2011 all over again! It's like we are playing a game of Russian roulette. I never know which spin of the cylinder will land on him picking up my calls.

I hate to admit it, but I envy the fact that my friends are able to do site visits with their partners. But more than anything, I envy the fact that whenever they need someone, their partner is there ready to be leaned on. I never thought I would look at another person's relationship and desire what they have. But it is not the big things I look at and want, it's the small things.

SCENE NINE:
THE WEDDING PLANNER

Venue – booked
Photographer – booked
Catering – booked
Dress – Purchased

There was not a detail of this wedding that was left unthought of. Planning this wedding helped distract me from the sadness I felt, and it soon became the best thing that could have happened to me.

I went from resenting Joseph for leaving, to thanking him for giving me something to distract my mind from my reality and the 101 problems I came to realise was in our relationship. I ignored the part of me that wished we could do the planning together and told myself that I was lucky that I could make all the decisions by myself.

As a young girl, I always dreamed of my Big Fat Nigerian Wedding. A celebration full of culture, food and good music. Most people dread the idea of having to figure out which of their 101 aunties, who aren't really their aunties by blood, but by affiliation, were going to make the guest list. Most people hated it; but not me. I couldn't wait for this to be the problem I was facing.

I wasn't the typical girl who complained about giving my parents a set number of invitees only for them to increase that number by at least 20%. I was just so happy that this was finally happening. I get to plan the day of my dreams and work towards a life of forever with the man I love. All the great plans I had conjured in my head will finally get the chance to be a reality. And not someone else's reality, mine. I had so many years full of dreams of how this process will be. But never did it occur to me that the man I would plan to marry would be over 3,000 miles away.

In the 19 months between the moment I said I do and the wedding date, I spent every moment planning my dream wedding. I say 'my' because for a large proportion of the planning, only my plans mattered. This was how I could cope with the disintegration of our relationship that was taking place behind the scenes.

I didn't have time to dwell on the fact that I missed Joseph. I ignored all the familiar behaviour from the last time he moved away, and I overlooked the internal feeling of fear every time I tried so desperately to capture his attention to no avail. I had one focus that would help me to get through it and that was planning this wedding.

For every one of the 19 months, I was occupied with activity after activity and left no moment of my day unaccounted for.

Some people drown their sorrows behind alcohol or drugs; I was drowning my sorrows behind the magazines, vendor meetings and venue viewings. It was no wonder that I found it so hard to deal with the demons I faced. Wedding planning became the drug I never knew I needed. Not the marriage, not my fiancé, but the wedding. At least if things were not 100% perfect behind the veil we put up to the world, the face our guests see behind my veil would be.

Somehow, I managed to fill up the lonely feeling with everything other than the solution. But things couldn't fill up the void. I kept running, hoping that my reality wouldn't catch up to me. But the more I ran, the more intensified the pain was. To everyone around me I was the most efficient bride there was. But the truth was, I gave myself a consolation prize in place of what should have been my winner's trophy. Consolations aren't for relationships with the man you are about to marry, there should be no 'runners up' award. I was continuously using phrases beginning with 'well at least we' or 'it could be worse'. When did least become the standard? When did anything better than the worst become the measure?

I gave myself consolation after consolation just so I could shield the sad reality that these were the loneliest months of my life.

I painted the picture of the couple I wanted the world to see. I cherished our good days because they were the moments I held onto in the hope that we could work. As time progressed, I was more interested in making sure that only our good days were presented to everyone watching. I constantly posted pictures on Instagram with captions detailing how much I missed him. One day it would be a throwback of the two of us in a matching outfit and the next it would be a screenshot of our far and few in between facetime calls. I never left it too long without posting him on social media. Now we were in separate countries, I needed our friends and families to think we were good. I didn't want anyone to know that with each passing day, our relationship was disintegrating.

I remember scrolling through my Instagram one day and realising that to the world, we were perfect.

I was my own lesson; if there is one reason I do not believe everything I see on social media; it is because of me.

***

No matter how occupied I became with planning this wedding, I never got use to the sadness. I spent so long being everything other than honest with myself and eventually, it became hard to differentiate what was right in a relationship and what was wrong.

I wonder now if it would have ever gotten this far if I had just been honest with myself that this was not right. I wonder if things would be different if I just opened up. It was not like I didn't have a great support network to guide me. Quite the opposite. I was surrounded by a great church family and even assigned a pre-marital counsellor; but all I did was tell them what they wanted to hear or allow them to draw a conclusion on our relationship based on the façade that we put up. I know that they must have suspected something whenever Joseph and I found excuses not to do the counselling or when we pushed meetings.

Growing up Nigerian, we were always told to deal with things in house. You don't tell people your business. You sort it out and keep it moving. This way of thinking is why so many people keep silent in the face of danger. When we see danger coming, our first instinct is to run and scream so we draw the attention of those around us to come and help. But why is it that when we see danger in our relationship, we stay silent?

Proverbs 15:22 tells us that without counsel plans fail, but with many advisers they succeed (ESV). We had a safe space to try and deal with our issues and we never used it. So instead of escaping the danger that was upon us, we walked right into it.

It was only so long before I noticed that the unhappy Joseph from 2010 never left. He just found better ways of hiding behind a stronger exterior. The man I loved was deeply broken. His sadness penetrated through every interaction we had together.

I tried so hard to ignore the voice inside of me that told me it would get worse if we don't get help. The mood swings scared me. One minute he was himself and the next he was a monster that began to speak to me in a way he never had. It frightened me to know that in the face of adversity, I had a man who would run from his issues and choose his partner as the dumping ground for his frustrations.

Some days, I made myself believe that it was normal for my partner to be this way. After all, I couldn't possibly understand what he was going through. This made is easier for me to pick up the pieces after he let out his anger on his family. It made turning the other cheek more doable when he called me selfish and wicked; amongst other names he would call me to get under my skin. I suppressed the inner voice of reason so much that all I could see was the man I knew he could be. But for how long would I see what he couldn't? I kept on affirming him like what I knew a good woman should do for the man she loves, I kept reminding him of who he was according to scripture. I did it all. But no attempts were fruitful enough for him to believe it too.

I thought that Joseph and I would be different. That unlike many of the marriages I have seen, happiness will be a major component to its success. But after a while I stopped holding on to this and started to wonder if happiness was possible in marriage. I stopped believing that a man could be so in love with his woman that he would protect her enough to know that what hurts him, hurts her. I turned a legitimate marital component into an unobtainable fairy-tale.

My thoughts were no longer founded on what the word of God said about marriage. I neglected the fact that when Adam saw Eve, he knew that he had seen himself. That he said 'this at last is bone of my bone and flesh of my flesh; she shall be called woman because she was taken out of me' (Genesis 2:23).

This scripture was not my reality. Joseph did not look at me and see him. I knew we were not married yet and technically these are all attributes shared between man and wife, but if I am to be his wife, then surely when he sees me he should see his future. And when I see him I should see mine too. But instead, all I could see what the past re-manifesting through a man who once promised me that this time would be different.

I even found comfort in hearing peoples horror stories of dysfunctional relationships, just so I could reassure myself that our relationship was normal.

As the days turned into weeks and weeks into months, being in a long-distance relationship did not get any easier. I firmly believed that it would until I began to find myself disappointed. Our arguments seemed to get worse with each one.

I knew that Joseph going back to Nigeria would cause a massive strain on our relationship. I knew it because he should have never gone back in the first place. Neither Joseph or I had peace with him moving back. This was later confirmed on numerous occasions by men and women of God made it clear to him that he shouldn't go back. He knew that going back when he did, posed a major risk to both our relationship and his walk with God. I was disappointed in him for not trying harder and having the faith to stay until the end of his visa. At least that way if he never got a job in London, we could all turn around and say he tried.

When he got offered the role in Nigeria, I never had peace about it. I know he thought it was me acting out of emotion and allowing my desire for him to cloud my judgment, but it was not. Something did not sit right with me. And I was right.

Shortly after he got to Nigeria, he waited on the employer to get in touch with his start date, but they never did. It was excuse after excuse but after each time he was in contact with them, he left feeling disappointed. At no point during this trying time did I ever have the thought 'if only he took me seriously' instead, I wanted to be there for him. But I didn't know how. At first, he tried not to shut me out completely but eventually the door was closed, and I never seemed to have the right key to open it again.

Some days I would pray and ask God how to deal with the

resistance that I felt from him. I just wanted to feel like he wanted me there. I wanted him to trust me enough to tell me how he was feeling. It was no wonder why I had days where I questioned whether I was cut out for this or not. I was so thankful that I had the wedding to help me get through the pain I shielded from the masses.

But I soon became so obsessed with planning my perfect wedding, that I lost sight of him and his needs and just how much our relationship needed attention so we could build a healthy marriage on a strong foundation. I took his attitude towards me as a direct attack when really it was his coping mechanism through his struggles and a cry for help. Distance was hard on him too. I at least had the wedding and my job to keep me occupied. He had nothing to distract him. Instead he had a job that fell through and a fiancé thousands of miles away.

Redundant.

When you pass through the waters, I will be with you; and though the rivers, they shall not overwhelm you: when you walk through fire you shall not be burned, and the flame shall not consume you. Isaiah 43:2

I remember the day I lost my job. He was the first person I called. It rang and rang and rang but there was no response. I had grown so use to him not answering my calls, but I rang anyway. I always thought that we had a connection. As strange as it sounds, I thought that because of this connection between him and I, he would just feel that I was not okay and something major was going on. So, unlike every other day, I would not need to fight for his attention.

On this day, the day my manager called me into her office and told me the company was restructuring and they will no longer need my services; I couldn't think about the last nine months of a toxic relationship. All I wanted was to hear his calm voice reassuring me everything will be okay. But he never answered the phone. Maybe the long distance had stifled our connection; or maybe the connection I imagined we had was just that – an imagination.

I kept on trying his line. With every call, I felt like I was losing air. We may not have had the most perfect relationship, but one thing was certain, he was always there for me when hard times hit.

After several call attempts, I sent him a message reading 'it's urgent'. Eventually he called me back. I don't know what was more painful; the fact that he wasn't there in my time of need or that it took an emergency to get my fiancé's attention.

I remember my mum once telling me *'it is in your time of need that you see who is really there for you'*. This was something that made it easy for me to determine who were my friends and who were my acquaintances. I remember thinking back to this when reflecting on the last few months. But I dismissed the feeling of wonder that crept up as I pondered on why it was at this moment that these words of wisdom from my mum came back to me.

Now I know that I was ignoring it. I knew that if I stayed there too long, I would realise that my then fiancé was no longer meeting the standard of friendship that he once did. Relationships change and it is our responsibility to address them when and if they do. Failure to address these issues run the risk of you completely ruining what you have built.

When he finally answered the phone and I told him the news, I heard his heart literally break for me. It was not the news he was expecting. It felt good to know that what hurt me hurt him. As horrible as the situation was, I hoped that this would bring us closer together. That we would use this opportunity to pray more and support one another as we tried to get ourselves back on our feet. In some respects, this was the case. But eventually, *my* issues became too hard for him to handle.

I remember applying to job after job and wondering why on earth I wasn't hearing back from anyone. I cried so hard in frustration. Naturally, my auto pilot move was to call my future husband. He would know what to say. But when I called him, he told me he had nothing. No words of encouragement, there was no 'it is going to be ok'. Nothing. Because right now, life has been hard for him and the one thing that kept him going was my happiness.

His exacts words to me were "I was ok because God had made things good for you. But now, everything is crumbling." The burden of guilt fell so heavily on me at that moment. For nine months I did not know that this was what was bringing him some form of joy. This guilt was soon followed by a heavy weight of responsibility to try and get my life back on track.

I was prepared for the times in our relationship where one

person needed to be lifted in prayer because the other person was down. I was well equipped for this and exercised it for majority of our relationship. But what happens when I am the one who needs him? Will he be there for me? Worst yet, what happens when both of us need holding up? What then?

Initially we began to argue less because other than the light morning conversations, we avoided each other. But when we did speak about the wedding and plans to come, it was disagreement after disagreement. Life was hard. My relationship was rocky and so was my career. Each day I lost count of the job applications I filled out and the 'no's' I received. But the ache of rejection from job application after job application, never compared to the ache of rejection from the man I was about to marry.

It became evident that the only thing holding us together was this commitment to make it down that aisle. The aisle became this idolised notion. How I wish I could tell my younger self that things don't just miraculously get better after 'I do'. Our determination to make it down the aisle meant that we carried on as normal and failed to deal with the many issues we had.

My individual prayer altar grew so cold. When I should have been running to God, I was disappointed in Him. How did He expect the two of us to start a life together when we were both unemployed and unhappy? Thankfully, the over planner in me had already paid the deposits for most of the things for our wedding so this bought us some time. But I was upset with life and I was upset with God.

***

Three months passed and I was still unemployed. Thankfully Joseph had managed to secure a job at a local organisation, and he seemed the happiest he had been since he left.

I couldn't imagine the sense of relief he must have felt when he heard the words 'you've been hired'. I remember the day he called me to tell me that he was made the offer. Tears of joy and relief rolled down my cheeks.

He was so excited to share this news with me. It felt good to hear him happy. It felt like God was slowly putting the pieces back together. I told myself that now he is employed his moods would be better and we could go back to how things were before he left.

Unfortunately, it was not going to be that easy. We had months of unresolved issues that we had not dealt with. It got to the point where it became easier to brush things underneath the rug and start afresh. We went back to speaking more frequently, bantering like we use to and we even began to pray together again. All the things I missed were now regular occurrences.

But not everything that is easier is best.

Eventually the heaps of mess that we swept under the rug piled up. It felt like we were tripping with every step. Joseph's post job honeymoon period was short lived. All of our issues around communication and my obsession with planning the perfect wedding was back at centre stage and the arguing continued.

Dear Diary,

What if.
What if how I feel isn't just about distance but everything going on in our relationship. I can't seem to shake off this gut feeling.
I never imagined drifting so far away from the man I plan to spend the rest of my life with.
Even with the excessive wedding planning, nothing could seem to distract me from the thought that the person I was about to do forever with didn't want to do forever with me.
Maybe I am being paranoid.
But what if I am not?
Lord, there are so many maybe's! But we have come too far for this not to end in the way everyone expects it to. I may not be happy right now, but I guess… I hope that once this season is behind us, I will be happy again.
And if I am not, then I will have to cross that bridge when I get there.

SCENE TEN:
TRADITIONAL WEDDING

It was a month to the date of our traditional wedding. Five months had passed and I was still unemployed. With the negative effect that distance was having on our relationship, I thought about applying for jobs in Nigeria. This was a big step for me. I was not sure of God's full purpose for my life, but one thing was for sure, Nigeria was not in it.

After only one interview, I was made an offer at a start-up company. I was ecstatic; finally, a job offer! I had never lived in Nigeria and I knew adjusting would be hard. But at least Joseph and I could be together. This would also mean that we wouldn't be spending the formative years of our marriage apart.

I told Joseph the news and he was pleased to begin with; until eventually, he forbid me from accepting the offer. I was taken aback. First of all, how dare he *forbid* me. And secondly why wasn't he happy? This could finally help us to resolve our issues. We would be together, employed and we could get the counselling we needed together instead of trying to do it over skype and combat the issue of poor wi-fi coverage in his house.

I was suspicious. Why didn't he want me there?

We went back and forth arguing, he said things to me that a man should never say to the woman he loved. This was not the first time he had called me out of my name and made me feel insignificant with his words. Eventually I confessed, "I can't do this anymore."

I was tired. Tired of trying and feeling like my efforts were wasted. Tired of always making excuses for him. Tired of feeling unwanted.

I felt so guilty for spurting those words out of my mouth. And it wouldn't be long before I would get a call from his mother, also asking me why I would say such a thing as that to her son. If I am honest with myself, I said it hoping that he would beg me to stay. I wanted a reaction from him. I wanted him to know that I could leave if he pushed me far enough.

But this backfired. Instead of getting the pleas I expected, I got an angry man who was ready to throw in the towel.

A few days passed and things were still up in the air. Our friends had no idea what was going on and neither did our extended family. His mum knew, his sister knew and that was it. Between them, they tried to make us see reason. I was the easier party to speak to. I wanted us to move past this. But it was interesting that at no point did his mother ask what had brought us to this point.

I guess the conversations worked because a few days later, Joseph wanted us to go ahead. He also asked me to move my ticket dates to Nigeria earlier so we could spend some time together before all of our guest arrived for the traditional wedding.

I flew to Nigeria earlier than planned and I am happy that I did. When I stepped out of the airport and saw him waiting for me, I was full of so much joy. I felt a sense of safety that I hadn't felt in a while. It was reassurance to me that our problems were distance led. Of course, they were not but, in that moment, it certainly did feel so.

The first week was amazing. We went on numerous dates, watched movies and we ate! Not the wisest of moves when you've got a wedding in a few weeks. None the less, we needed that time to remind ourselves that before anything, we were friends.

I knew that eventually we would have to speak about everything. We thought that we could at least try to resolve things in person before our friends arrived and noticed the hostility between us. Deep down, I knew that there were issues deeper than being distant. The distance held a mirror to our incompatibilities and our personal flaws. Us being apart was only temporary. We knew we would eventually live in the same country and so we had a plan to work towards. The real issue was that I stopped feeling secure in my relationship.

Instead of dealing with the real matter at hand, I was full of excuses. For every issue, I made an excuse. It wasn't us who had the problem I thought, it was our situation. 'If we were in the same country' or 'if I was working' then things would be better.

Truthfully every issue we were having in our relationship were not issues we hadn't faced in the past. They were accumulated problems that we never fully dealt with. There was so much mess to get through that I didn't see the point of starting now. We were surviving in spite of a heaped rug of unresolved issues we were hiding. So instead of trying, I resumed life as normal and so did he. We settled for surviving because to us, thriving did not feel like it was an option.

I wanted that to change. Now we had nowhere to hide. It was just me and him in the room with our problems. We were at his house in Lagos when I first began to bring up how the past year of us being separate had made me feel. To my surprise, he was receptive. Eventually he began to open up about his concerns too. We were making progress and the moment we started unpicking at it, the lighter things seemed to get. But we couldn't resolve all of our issues in a few weeks and we knew that. We promised ourselves that when we were together, we would pray more. We even set time out to fast. But of course, we didn't. We had not been in each other's company since my last visit to Lagos seven months before. We were so caught up in emotions that after that day, we parked our issues to enjoy the moments. Why would we waste the precious time we have together dealing with issues when we could be making up for lost time. This mindset is not one that anyone going into marriage should have. And we would soon pay the price.

***

The countdown to our traditional wedding began.

The more time we spent with one another, the harder pretending everything was okay became. As we drew closer to the day, the tension between us grew. We could barely get through an entire day without disagreeing on one thing or another.

By my third week in Lagos, most of our guests had arrived. For many, it was their first time seeing Joseph since he had moved back to Nigeria. I thought that the excitement of seeing our friends would relieve some of the pressures we were facing. And for a while it did. But gradually, our disagreements became so bad that no matter how we tried to hide it from them, they picked up on it. For the most part, they never mentioned it. But I can still remember the day one of my best friends, Ling asked me why I did not seem happy.

She had always known us to be so happy together. I tried my hardest not to involve my friends in our issues, so I put on a smile and replied, "it's just wedding stress". Other than the few days she spent with us in Lagos, Ling had no reason to believe that we had any issues. So, she believed me, and I was glad she did.

I knew my friends would not judge me for having issues in my relationship but I was so used to maintaining the image that we were your model long distance relationship couple that I didn't want the façade to be revealed when we were so close to the quitting line.

I never accounted for the fact that in the years we had been together, we had both changed. For some reason I expected that as we grew, we would grow together and be in sync. But for us, we seemed to be growing and repelling. Physically being with him for the first time in months made our differences more noticeable. I saw sides to Joseph and myself that I had never seen in the years we had been together. The side of him that disrespected me in the presence of his mother and the side of me that would accept it. The side of him that would display blatant patriarchy on the verge of misogyny in the presence of his friends, and the side of me that mistook compliance for submission.

It was one thing for him and I to be butting heads but for him to publicly disrespect me was another? This was a line he hadn't crossed in the past and the more I sat there and allowed it, the further away from the line he became.

As I look back in hindsight, I can see how God was revealing to me everything that would pose an issue in marriage. But at the time, I saw it as one more thing to conceal in the hopes that it would change. 'He was not this way before' I would tell myself.

I remember my friend once telling me that whatever you see before marriage, expect it intensified ten times more in marriage. But instead of thinking in a way that could prepare me for what may never change, I remained wishful that it would. For the next few days, I spent my mornings worrying about how I would get through each day. I had to smile in front of our loved ones, all the while knowing that something was not right.

The day before our traditional wedding, Joseph and I we were barely speaking. I was at a hotel close to the venue with a few of my friends the night before. I had booked my own room which gave me enough time to rest and pray before the big day. As I prayed, I knew that it was not right to go ahead with this when we both had so much animosity in our hearts. So, I sent him a message in an attempt to clear the air. He responded only moments later telling me that he loved me and that we should get some rest before our big day.

The message felt flat. Like an obligatory response of acknowledgment.

How I managed to go through it knowing how heavy my heart was is still something I question until this day. Was I so consumed with saving face that I gave up the opportunity to save my heart? In the presence of over 500 guests, we went through the traditional wedding.

To our friends and family, it was a beautiful celebration. And don't get me wrong, it was. The beautiful colours of the hall, our cake, the outfit. Everything came together perfectly. Everything aside from the couple that is.

As I looked at my groom, I could see that behind that smile he plastered on his face, was a man who was broken. I wished that as I danced up to him that he smiled from the heart and told me I was beautiful. But he didn't. I knew just like me, he was so torn. He wanted things to be better, but he couldn't see how. I could see that he loved me. I knew that had not changed. And from the beginning of our relationship until that day, it was not the way he treated me or the words he said that made me so sure of the love he had for me. It was the way he looked at me.

The little sparkle in his eyes when I made him happy and when I made him sad. And now, even in his confusion, the sparkle was still there. Even when I couldn't physically see him, somehow, I knew that that twinkle never went away. It was the twinkle in his eye that made me see the star in him. He was once my bright light at the end of a difficult day. My rare gem in the midst of many. It was that twinkle in his eye as I looked up at him that reminded me why I had to fight for our love.

On the day of our traditional wedding, a determination arose in me to fight for us. I knew that our relationship was one that started off well but took many bad turns. I knew that there was a time that I had overwhelming peace that he was the one for me. Everything I was doing up until that point was not working. Pretending everything was ok when it wasn't, was not working. Trying to figure out how I could please him, speaking to his family members to get advice was no longer working. Don't get me wrong, there is a place for that. But when it comes to the person you want to marry and the union you are about to go through, you must not underestimate the importance of prayer.

I felt so strongly that God let us get to this point so we could see just how much we needed Him to get through this.

Who knows him better than the One who created him? Who could love me enough to lead me in the path that I should go? The answer was right in front of me the whole time. I was afraid that it was too late. I couldn't change the time I spent running but I could control what I would do moving forward. For the next 4 months, I contended for my relationship. Storms arose but I never stopped praying. In those 4 months I learnt how to strip myself of self. I surrendered every part of me to God and I became so intimate with the Holy spirit that nothing phased me.

In the eyes of our family, we were now officially husband and wife. Although we were set on the church wedding being our official wedding date, we appeased our traditions and parents. The night of the traditional wedding, I packed my bags and moved to Joseph's family home.

It was the first night we would share a bed together.

A part of me thought that maybe if we were physically intimate things would get better for us. But we made a promise to one another that we would wait until our official wedding night to consummate our marriage. I was tempted to give in. I even packed some sexy lingerie. But I didn't need to. The buzz from the wedding meant that we were on cloud nine.

Our final wedding guests flew back to their various destinations five days after the traditional wedding which gave us much needed time alone. I spent the next two weeks with Joseph working through some of our issues and being intentional about enjoying each other's company. He planned dates just for the two of us; each day we did something new. Date nights were always special with Joseph. When he moved to Nigeria, I missed our weekly dates. Joseph's romantic side meant that our dates may not have always been the fanciest but my oh my, were they special.

Spending time with him like that again was everything I could have hoped for. On my last day in Lagos, he took me to the restaurant we went to on my first trip to Nigeria after he moved in 2010. We sat in the same section of the restaurant and on the same table. It was perfect. I was getting back the version I knew of the man I loved.

Everything inside of me wanted to extend my trip a few more days. His birthday was coming up and since we couldn't spend his last birthday together, this one would have been extra special. Aside from that, even though things had been good for the past two weeks, we were still working through our issues. But I had to go back. I was now in my sixth month of being unemployed. Joseph and I could not reach an agreement about me taking the job in Lagos, so I had no option other than to turn it down. I was devastated by this, but I felt like had to honour his request even if I didn't understand it.

I continued applying for Jobs in London while I was in Nigeria and I managed to secure a few interviews. So, I flew back home.

At first things between us were great. I decided to not let everything with the job, and the pre traditional wedding drama get in the way with the progress we were making. I was trying to remain optimistic that it would stay that way. But just as I suspected, things changed. It was like there was a lingering spirit sent to cause division between us not only geographically but emotionally.

The usual behaviour crept up. The delayed responses to my messages, the unanswered calls. Anyone would think I should be used to it. But of course, I was not. Whenever I mentioned it, we argued, so I gave up mentioning it. When I tried to get him to agree on things for the wedding, he would get angry, so I went back to making decisions alone.

Even with dedicating time to daily prayers and weekly fasts, we still argued. Why could we never argue well? Why did our arguments always feel like reoccurring prison sentences with no possibility of parole?

I suggested everything from praying together again to fasting to joint counselling. But instead, he wanted to do his counselling session separate from me. He agreed to prayer but separate from me. And when I sent him scriptures and prayer points for our joint fast, he said he will do his prayer points separate from me. For a man who was about to take vowels to cleave and become one flesh with me, the signs were loud and clear that he was not ready to do life with another person by his side.

Two weeks into my return to London, and I couldn't see how I could win this battle. I began to feel like my being repulsed him and instead of walking away or speaking up, I continued to fake it, hoping to one day make it. I was determined not to give up. I kept pressing in but the more I pressed the more I felt that things were getting worse. I was permanently walking on eggshells. Still I continued to pray hoping that one day things would turn around. And in some respects, it did. Emotionally I became stronger, I finally got a great job and I was closer to God than ever.

Everything around me was bearing fruit. That is everything except for my relationship. It was by far the most important thing to me in the physical realm and it was the one thing that I felt God was not making right.

Now I see that God was making me stronger and pruning me in areas so that I could grow. But the more he tugged on my relationship, the more I resisted. I thought that I could out pray God's blatant signs that something was wrong. I told myself that the distance was the issue. When I was with him, we were doing better. I told myself this so much that after one of our many fall outs, I booked a ticket to Nigeria.

No matter how much I wanted to get married to him, even I knew that we couldn't get married in the state that we were. Things were worse than they had ever been. So six weeks before our wedding date, I booked the next available flight to Lagos. He had no idea I was coming until I was already on board. Of course he was not happy that at a time that we barely had the financial resources I was flying several thousand miles to go and see him. But money was the least of our problems.

I landed at 5 am the following morning. His mother sent her driver to pick me up from the airport. The whole journey to his family home, I wondered what was going to happen. This trip was the make or break of our relationship. Whatever happens on this day, would determine if we go ahead with the white wedding or not.

We pulled into his compound and it was still fairly dark outside. When I got into the house, I went upstairs to greet his parents and then made my way down to his room. I knocked on the door for a few minutes before he eventually answered. Seeing him made me want to fight for this even more. And I hoped that when he saw me, he would feel the same. And I was right. The first day, we spent hours speaking and mapping out what went wrong. The conversation got so heated that there were so many moments that I thought he would walk out on me.

But the truth was, we needed it. We needed to let it all out. There was so much uncertainty in our relationship. Where would we live? How long would we be a part after we got married? Could we really survive this?

With everything up in the air we needed to make a decision. We never envisioned ourselves being in a situation where we lived in two different continents with no idea when we would be able to live with one another. Clearly, we were not working being apart and the truth is we still had a road ahead of us that consisted of him and I married and in two separate countries. I had grown up in an environment where long distance marriages were normalised. But I saw the strain it had on my family and I didn't want that for myself. We knew it wouldn't be forever but what if our plans for a spousal visa failed? Could we survive another six months like this? Do I pick up my life and move to Nigeria even though I had the opportunity to and he said no?

I knew that I was willing to risk it all if risking it all meant that I had him. No matter how much I said it, he never really seemed to believe it in the past. But after I flew all that way to see him, I believe it hit him just how much I was in this for the long haul.

After what felt like hours, we finally went to sleep. He got up early the next morning and went to work. While he was at the office, I spent time in the house praying and covering the atmosphere in the blood of Jesus. Because let's be real, there had to be some kind of spirit flying around in that place.

While he was at the office, I received a message from Joseph saying be ready at six. Thankfully I had packed a cute dress with me as you do when you are trying to reconcile with your fiancé. I wore the dress, flung on a pair of heels and met him outside.

"Wow, you look beautiful!" he said, opening the passenger door for me.

He drove us to an Italian restaurant on the Lagos island and I couldn't help but think back to only a few years before when he took me to an Italian restaurant in order to win me back over. We ate our pasta and of course, I liked his better, so in true Joseph fashion, he swapped his plate with mine. After we finished our meals, we headed to our favourite karaoke spot.

Joseph loved Karaoke and I loved cheering him on from the side-lines as he sang one of the many ballads in his song list. The night was everything I could have hoped for. When we got in the car and drove home, Joseph looked at me.

"I want us to work." He confessed. "In six weeks, we are getting married so let's do all we can to make this right."

I was so relieved to hear these words come out of his mouth. I left for London the following day and prayed that unlike the other times, this time would be different. We would be good for more than a few weeks and communication would remain constant. And it was. I started my new job the following week and each day things between Joseph and I seemed to be getting better.

Part 3

SCENE ELEVEN:
JILTED

April 4th 2016

It had been 24 hours since I last heard from Joseph. He was supposed to be on a plane tomorrow. The wedding was only a few days away and so many obstacles prohibited him from being here sooner. Finally, there was a silver lining. A way for him to get here.

But when it seemed like he would make his way to me, I was hit with news that changed everything. I received a text message from his mum. A message that ended with the line *'I am sorry Sarah, April 9th is an impossibility.'*

I read the message over, and over, again. Maybe if I kept reading it, the content of the message would miraculously change. Was it possible that somehow I misread the words on my screen and that the message was sent to the wrong person? He wouldn't do this to me. He couldn't. And through his mum?

In what life does someone get told their wedding is not happening by their fiancé's mum and in a text message?

Everything about that day felt like a nightmare that I kept reliving. The feeling of disbelief coupled with the hurt that filled me made it hard for me to come to terms with what was happening. Standing up, I walked blindly to my parent's room; gripping the phone tightly. With an outstretched hand, wordlessly, I gave my mum the phone, so she could read what I could not bring myself to say.

As she read the words on the screen, I became numb. Absent minded, I glanced around the room, wondering *'is this really my life? Am I really here? Is this really happening?'*

I saw my mum pick up her phone and dial a number. She walked over to the other side of the room and raised the phone to her ear. I could see her mouth moving but I couldn't hear what she was saying. It was like I was experiencing life with no sound. Eventually my mother got off the phone and walked me back to my room; holding me all the while.

She got an overnight bag out of the cupboard and began to pack a few of my items. At the time, I didn't know why or where I was going. All I knew was that my life was breaking into little pieces. Pieces too small for me to pick up and put together on my own.

When she was done packing, we made our way downstairs, got into the car and she drove off. I had no idea where we were going. I didn't think to ask. My mind was still on the text – trying to process it. As I sat in the passenger seat silently, a notification came through on my phone. It was the bridal store.

'Good news Sarah, we can get the dress alterations done by Thursday at 12pm.'

And that is when it hit me. It was in that moment that it dawned on me that I wouldn't be collecting my dress because there would be no wedding on Saturday.

Still experiencing life with no sound; warm tears fell down my cheeks as I wept silently, hoping that my mum would not notice. I closed my eyes tightly hoping that I could sleep and make the pain disappear. If I closed my eyes tightly enough, I could sleep away this bad dream of my current reality.

Eventually the car stopped. I opened my eyes, slowly taking in my surroundings. We were outside my best friend's apartment. As my mum pulled up to the car park, she was waiting for me outside. Unbeknown to me, my mum had called her and told her she needed her to look after me. We got out of the car and my mum embraced me in the way only a mother could. At the comfort of her warm embrace, I rested my head on her shoulder and began to cry.

"Why is this happening to me, mummy? Why?"

From the corner of my eye I could see my best friend holding her tears back as she came to embrace me in my mother's arms. I didn't want my mum to leave but she knew she had to get me out of the house. In a few hours we would have to inform our guests and in true Nigerian fashion, there would be floods of visitors at our door with care packages and well wishes. My mum knew I couldn't handle that. So, like any good mother she protected me and took me to where she knew I would be safe.

My best friend Kevwe and I had been friends since the age of eleven. Even when I moved away for university, she and I remained best friends. We had been through so much together and supported one another through the highs and the lows. But nothing could have prepared us for this.

I was so ashamed. We were supposed to be preparing for a high. My wedding day. Instead she had to hold me up through the hardest trial of my life. How could I be putting my friends and family through this?

Kevwe got my bags out of the car and she walked me up to her flat. My mum followed behind, got me settled in and hugged me as she said bye.

"Call me if you need anything, or if you want me to come back and get you." she said as she approached the door.

I looked up and gave her a nod of acknowledgment. And she left. To my right was Kevwe. She stayed beside me for what felt like hours. I was so embarrassed to tell her that the man I told her made me happy had made me the saddest I had ever been. I spent so long pretending that our issues were fixable that I couldn't bear to look my friend in the eyes. I knew she suspected something was not right between us when she came to take me out for my birthday a few months before.

Kevwe, Ling and Tiffany came to take me out. When they arrived, Kevwe noticed I had been crying. She could always see when I was faking it. I promised her I was okay and that I was just missing Joseph. But she knew it was more. But in true Kevwe style, she gave me my space hoping that one day I would tell her what was really wrong. I never imagined that that one day would be this day.

Eventually I stopped avoiding eye contact. And when I did, I saw a friend who would never judge me for the mistakes I made.

"What am I going to do Kevwe?" I asked with tears rolling down my face.

She took my right hand and held it in her palms and said, "For now you are going to sit here and do nothing. Whatever you need to do, I will do it."

I laid my head on the arm of the sofa, shut my eyes and I cried myself to sleep.

***

I had to tell my bridesmaids what had happened. I needed it to come from me and not from anyone else. At 8pm that night, I composed a message to the group chat. It wasn't until 20 minutes after I composed the message that I managed to summon the courage to press send.

When I pressed send, I felt a blanket of shame overwhelm me. I made sure that I asked them all to give me space until further notice. I knew that if I didn't, they would inevitably attempt to call me or drive over to see me. Of course, they all messaged me back. But I couldn't bring myself to respond.

Once I told the bridesmaids, I waited a few hours to send a mass email to our wedding guests. This one was going to be hard. The message was going to go out to every person that RSVP'd. Everyone from our parent's friends to our friends and family. There was a rush of anxiety taking over me and all the while, I could see it in Kevwe's eyes that she was wondering why I had to be the one to do this. Where was Joseph?

As I sat there, phone in hand and heart shattered, like Kevwe, I wondered the same thing.

It was now 10pm and I didn't know whether Joseph had informed his family and friends about what was going on. I needed to get on top of this before word got out.

As I typed the message, I couldn't help but think about my family who flew over from all over the world. So much money had been spent by the ones who loved us, now the wedding would not be taking place.

I tried to think of the best way to tell everyone the wedding would not proceed on Saturday. How could I let them know while simultaneously telling them how much we appreciate them? I appreciated them.

Eventually I figured out what to say and gave the phone to Kevwe so she could read it through before I hit send.

Kevwe took the phone from me and began to read the message

out loud.

Evening all. Firstly, I wanted to say a big thank you to you all for your love and support to myself and Joseph. Unfortunately, due to matters outside of our control, Saturday will be postponed. We are truly sorry for all of the inconvenience caused. We ask that everyone please keep us in your prayers. We will be in touch with updates. Once again sorry for all the inconvenience caused and thank you for your support.

Sending out that mass message to all of our guest is still one of the hardest things I think I have had to do. And it was something I had to do alone. The day was drawing to an end, and Joseph had still made no contact.

From this day forward, my life as I knew it was no longer the same. I ran away from the world thinking that somehow avoiding human contact would restore my world to what it was before he tried to break it. I wondered how I would ever be able to face my friends, family and church. How would anyone ever look at me the same way? What would I say when they asked me what happened?

It was hard to believe that the problems with travel documents were nothing more than a cover up. A part of a bigger plan to end what we had. I couldn't help but think that the real reason he watched me plan this wedding and never contributed was not because he couldn't, but it was to stop him from getting invested in a day that he knew would never happen. Was I the last person to know that April 9th 2016 was never going to be the date of our wedding?

How could I be so blindly in love and so desperately in need of our picture perfect relationship that I couldn't see what was in front of me?

Surely if this was legitimate and there was no way he could travel down he would have called me and told me himself. He, like me, would have been broken and we would have gone through this together.

But instead, I was alone dealing with the aftermath and barely holding on to my sanity.

As we began to inform the vendors that the wedding was no longer taking place that Saturday, I felt myself slowly deteriorating. Thankfully my friend and coordinator picked this up and did it for me. I had built such a strong relationship with all of my vendors that I couldn't bear to face them.

All the months I spent planning and using this wedding to mask my pain and for what?

The day that would only be spoken about in pity. A day that I thought would make it all worth it became the most daunting day of my life. A day that reminded me of a betrayal I never thought I would experience. He left me in a state of brokenness. At my lowest point, I was able to see that no matter how much his friends and family told me I was one of them, when push came to shove, I wasn't. I can count how many of his family members contacted me after the wedding got called off. People I had spent the last 6 years calling my family showed me that only those ready to battle in adversity can be called a brother.

***

Like everyone else, I didn't know what was next for us. I wanted to believe that him not getting on that plane was not because he didn't want to be with me. I kept telling myself that there were issues with travel documents and in due course we would get married. Even when he neglected me, I still wanted us to work. With Joseph I threw away what I knew to be right because what I wanted was right there in front of me. What I wanted was him.

As I sat alone with my thoughts, I realised that the bandage I was using to hide the deepness of every place he cut me, was no longer sufficient.

The unhealed wounds from the fights we had in 2014 could no longer be concealed. The anxieties that I tried to wish away in 2015 were only getting deeper. And in 2016 the fear that he would one day leave me eventually became my reality. With every untreated wound, our love became infected. Every undiagnosed concern multiplied until it invaded my entire being. This was an infection that had a limited time before it either killed me or I killed it.

SCENE TWELVE:
THE AFTERMATH

Two days later I went back home. My dad had flown back in from Abuja and I needed to see him. I wanted him to know that his little girl was okay. Of course I wasn't, but I was afraid of what he would do if he knew that. He and my brothers took it as hard as I thought they would and I knew the only way they would have any sense of comfort, is if they knew I was okay.

Feeling the emotions of my parents was too much for me to handle. On the one hand my mum was comforting me and on the other my dad was so busy trying to fix it that I became overwhelmed.

It had been less than 24 hours since I came back home and I knew that I couldn't stay there anymore. I knew I couldn't look my mother in the face while she tried to stay strong for me. My mum has always been my rock in human form. I could see the pain she tried so hard to conceal every time she looked at me. If she could take my pain away, I knew she would. And if I could make her smile again, I would. I know my mum was not disappointed in me. But I was disappointed in myself. Disappointed that I allowed this kind of shame to be brought to my family. Especially after everything she had endured for the sake of my brothers and I. This was supposed to be a day where she could see the rewards of her labour. The day she sees the girl she gave birth to become the woman she raised.

Through the planning process my mum and I were like best friends. It wasn't just my wedding it was hers too. She even hired her own wedding planner. Every now and again we would buttheads but it would always end with endless laughs.

I hated that I couldn't see that proud smile. Instead I saw hurt.

I knew I couldn't stay in the house for much longer. Between the pain of my mother and watching my dad pretend that everything was okay, I couldn't bear waking up the next morning to face what seemed like the grief of my family.

Early the next morning, I woke up at 3am and began to pack.

My friends had booked a room at a local hotel near the reception venue. With the wedding no longer taking place that weekend, they asked me if I wanted to stay there and clear my head. I will never forget this act of love. I thought going to the hotel was just to get away. But God had additional plans. It was that very weekend that I started to write. I didn't know what I was writing for, but writing was all I could do.

As I look back in hindsight, years on, I see that even though it felt like I was surrounded by so much hurt and pain, God placed people in my life to surround me with love that showed me His heart through mankind. My support system personified Provers 17:17

"A friend loves at all times, and a brother is born for adversity."

***

By the time I finished packing, it was 4am; I had 11 hours until check in. The wheels in my mind churned as I wondered what to do. I knew that if I waited, my parents would convince me to stay at home which I did not want.

While everyone was sound asleep in the house. I remember carrying my bag as I tiptoed through the corridor to get down the stairs without being heard. Before I left, I composed a message to my brother.

The message was not a detailed one. It was simply informing him that I would be checking in to a hotel for a few days. I told him to tell my parents not to worry; I knew that they would either way. But at this point I had to focus on what was best for me. And every day I faced my family, the thoughts of escaping the pain I was feeling became darker and darker.

I made it downstairs without anyone hearing me, hurried to my car, loaded my bags, and began to drive. I drove around for a few hours before I eventually went to the hotel. I couldn't tell you what was going through my head when I was driving. All I recall is that I had 11 hours till check in.

I drove around for two hours before I finally made my way to the hotel. I still had nine hours before check-in, but I took my chances and made my way to the hotel to see if I could get in sooner. The rooms were all fully booked and I was asked me to come back at 12 to see if a room would become available.

That was still six hours away. I couldn't wait six hours. I decided to drive to a hotel not too far and see if they had a room available. Thankfully they did. I got myself checked in, switched off my phone and made my way to my room.

As I swiped my card through the door, I walked into the room and laid my bag on the floor next to the wardrobe. As I lifted my head up, I saw my reflection in the mirror opposite me. Staring back at me was the face of a woman who I could no longer recognise. It wasn't the strong, happy, beautiful Sarah I once knew. This woman was deflated, I was repulsed by my own reflection.

Falling to my knees, I wept. I was so exhausted. I felt mentally drained and physically worn out yet somehow, the pain of my inner being found enough energy to cry out to God like never before.

It was just me, these four walls and God. I had so many questions to ask, so many things to say. I tried so hard to let it all out but the tears forming, and my shortness of breath prevented anything from coming out. Picking myself up from the ground, I managed to walk towards the bed.

On the bed side table, there was a notepad and a pen. I sat down on the bed and I began to write. I kept writing until I filled each page of the note pad. I filled each page with my deepest thoughts and soaked them with my tears. As I wrote, I could feel an overwhelming presence with me holding me up when my feet almost failed me.

I knew it could only be the Holy spirit comforting me.

Before I knew it, the words on the paper became the murmurs on my lips. I began to speak out to God. I may not have known exactly what to do but I knew exactly what I needed and at the moment, that was the help I needed. I needed help with the battle taking place in my mind; help to make sense of what was going on.

Help to make it through another day. And as I spoke out to God, I knew that I was not alone. The overwhelming peace in the midst of the storm overtook me. I may not have known how, but I somehow knew that this too would pass. And even in the midst of the waves tossing me to and fro, I had confidence that God was right there, holding me up.

For the next few hours, I remained in a foetus position on the bed in the hotel room and wept at the feet of the Master. I did this until I had to eventually leave and make my way to the hotel my friends booked for me. I had very little words left to say but I knew God heard the words of my tears.

"The righteous cry out, and the Lord hears, and delivers them out of their troubles." Psalm 34:17

***

When I arrived at the hotel that would be my home for the next two days, I ordered some food, got into bed and went to sleep. I woke up in the middle of the night anxious about how I would feel in the morning. It was the eve of what should have been our wedding day. I had the day planned down to the tee.

My bridesmaids and I would all stay at the same hotel while the groomsmen and my groom stayed at another. I should be fast asleep by now but in reality, I pictured myself up laughing away with Kevwe and Ling until we would eventually fall fast asleep until we were woken up by the alarm.

Ling would get up first. But not to get ready. She would sneak out and make her way to her room and try to get in a few more hours of sleep. I would be second to get up. I would go, get in the shower and pray by myself while I daydreamed about how my hair and make-up would turn out. Then my coordinator would knock on my door with a clipboard in her hand and the pre-approved schedule I put together for the bridal party.

I thought about every detail for the morning of our wedding. But now none of that mattered. I tried to push these thoughts to the back of my mind. I went back to sleep and woke up on Saturday morning feeling exactly how I thought I would: miserable.

I knew that there was nothing I could do to change what I was going through. I hoped that on this day, the day our wedding was supposed to happen, I would get a call from Joseph telling me that everything will be okay. But I never got that call. Since the wedding had been postponed, he had barley spoken to me. I couldn't understand how or why he wasn't feeling what I was feeling.

I knew if I stayed in that hotel alone for any longer, I would lose all sense of what was right and wrong. I couldn't trust myself to ignore the thoughts that told me that I was worthless. So eventually, I picked up my phone and sent Kevwe a message with the hotel address. Within hours I heard a knock on the door. As I walked to the door 5 of my closest friends were there armed with goodies, smiles and love. It was that knock that saved me from drowning that night. That day the love of my friends reminded me that I was worthy of another person's love. Together, safe in the love of their laughter and presence, I found comfort in my hotel room that night.

Just like the previous night, I was unable to sleep. I woke up in the middle of the night, but this time it was a different feeling. This time I felt overwhelmed by human love. For so long I allowed the love I was missing from my partner to shape my views on how I was loved. As I continued to think about this love, I had a vision of me seated at church.

In the bible we see that the church was the bride of Christ. At first, I thought this vision was a reminder to me that Christ loved me. But it was more than that.

I felt so strongly in my spirit that God was telling me I had to go to church the next day. I prayed and prayed and fought and fought against it. I wonder now why I tried to fight it. As if God would ever tell me not to be in His presence. I knew if I didn't turn up no one would have been surprised. But I could feel that it was more than me going as a sign of commitment or even honour. It was me going as a step towards breaking through.

The weight of shame I felt was almost destroying me. And now God wanted me to confront it. I knew questioning God in that moment wouldn't help because He is all I had. When Sunday came, I built up courage and obediently went to church. It took me thirty minutes to get out of the car and walk upstairs to the church hall. In those thirty minutes, I tried to convince myself that going home was not the answer. I thought of every possible question I could be asked and all of the answers I could give. Thirty minutes and lots of thoughts later, I messaged my dear friend Kara and told her I was here.

When Kara had been at the hotel the previous night, I had told her that I would be coming to church in my own time; I doubt she thought 'my own time' would be so soon. She responded to my text asking if she should come and meet me outside. I considered it for a moment, before deciding against the thoughtful gesture. If she did it would draw more attention to me; so I replied "no" and made my way up to the sanctuary.

As I walked through the doors, I felt many eyes on me from every direction. My feet felt like heavy weights as I walked towards a seat. The attention quickly turned from the Bishop's sermon to me. Well at least that is what it felt like. Avoiding any eye contact, I sat in my seat with my head down, wondering why I even bothered to come. This didn't feel like courage to me. I wasn't bold. I couldn't even raise my head up and look at the person right beside me. I wanted so badly for the service to be over so I could pick up my bag, head to the door and leave.

As it was coming to the end of the sermon, I felt what appeared to be a heavy burden being lifted from me. I won't pretend that I can adequately explain what it was or even that I could say that I felt better. But what I did know is that I felt lighter. It was a similar feeling to what I experienced in the hotel room. I felt like I was no longer carrying this burden by myself. And for the first time in the six days since the wedding was called off, I didn't feel ashamed. It was then that I realised the power of healing in fellowship.

I felt like I was pulling strength from the body of Christ without myself or even them noticing. This instrumental moment in my healing process came as a result of obedience even when it didn't make sense. My weakness was exchanged for Gods perfect strength so even when I felt too weak to fight, I knew the one inside of me was always ahead of me.

Prior to this moment, I planned that I would take time off church. But this encounter led me to realise that the spiritual motivation that comes from corporate fellowship will be instrumental to me making it through.

'This is not the time to pull away and neglect meeting together, as some have formed the habit of doing. In fact, we should come together even more frequently, eager to encourage and urge each other onward as anticipate that day dawning.'
Hebrews 10: 24

I am thankful for the friends God blessed me with. Each and every one of them supported me in different ways. I was blessed with many friends and it was in this dark hour that I would see why God placed them all in my life.

As much as I could feel God moving, there were so many days I couldn't pray. And on those days, I am thankful for my friend turned sister, Rev Kara. Although I met Kara at church, she was originally Joseph's friend before she and I became so close. Because she and Joseph had such a good relationship, it was often easier to speak to Kara about some of the things I couldn't speak to my other friends about. Kara's response to everything was always to listen and to follow it up with prayer. Like clockwork, Kara picked up the phone and called me every day to pray. Some days I would sit on the phone silently while she prayed for me and over me. I believe more than ever that those prayers were instrumental to me going through this season but more so, it was exactly what I needed for the hurt that was still yet to come.

A week had passed, and Joseph had not called me. On numerous days I called him and received no answer. On one particular day, he answered the phone and he told me that he would call me back. Of course he never did. I stopped making excuses for him. What excuse could I possibly give for a man who was neglecting the woman he was supposed to love at such a crucial time? I knew that this was not a case of him being busy or leaving the phone in the other room. This was intentional. He was punishing me in the way he knew would hurt me the most. A punishment I was used to. He was punishing me with his silence.

The difference between now and all the other times he did this, is I didn't know what I was being punished for.

He ignored my calls while continuing life as normal. I thought that this punishment would last a week or two at the most. After all, who can go that long and willingly not speak to the person they love. Not for one moment did I think this punishment would be one that carried on for 21 days. Over these 21 days he made it clear to me that he could live life normally without me. He was on; snapchat, Instagram, WhatsApp; you name it.

But somehow, he never had the time to call me. I realised then why it was easy for me to make the excuses or to act like this behaviour was justifiable. It was easy because the thought of accepting rejection was one too hard for me to bare. Of all the emotions that a man has ever made me feel, the feeling of rejection is one that he promised he will never make me feel again. So every time I saw it creep up in our relationship, I would rather blame the situation for making me feel rejected and not him. I existed in this relationship feeling the very rejection he promised to shelter me from. But through my own dismissal of my emotions, I gave this feeling a different name.

Mentally I was in way too deep to ignore what was in front of me. The burden felt too heavy for me to carry. How could he be doing this to me? What could I have done that was so bad that he would make me feel like this? Every day I spoke to Kara right before I went to sleep and my Bishop every morning when I woke up. The strength people saw in me day in and day out was because they spoke life through the word of God before I laid my head to bed, and when I rose up in the morning. I did this until I felt strong enough to do it myself.

My community upheld me when I needed them the most. Leaning on them helped my faith to increase. Somehow, seeing their faith encouraged me that there was an end to this ordeal. Irrespective if how it looked, there was an end. And God knew the end right from the beginning. I will be honest and say there were times that I wanted to send mammoth length messages or even book a flight to go and see him. These were all irrational thoughts driven by a broken heart. My community held me accountable by giving me Godly counsel in order to make Godly decisions.

Each day I was reminded of what the Apostle Paul quite rightly said, '*we do not look at the troubles we can see now, rather we fix our gaze on things that cannot be seen. For the things we can see now will soon be gone, but the things we cannot see, will last forever.*' 2 Corinthians 4:18.

As the days rolled into weeks, I held on to the hope that I was not alone. That this deep wound will one day stop bleeding and produce a scar with a story that will not just change my life but maybe help others. So, I kept pushing. The more I pushed the harder it seemed to feel. And sometimes this scared me. But I never stopped. My faith gave me the strength that anxiety never could.

'He only is my rock and my salvation, my fortress; I shall not be shaken.'
Psalm 62:6.

Dear Diary,

I am at a crossroad and I don't know what to do.

I take one step towards him and I am left bruised with memories of the past.

I take one step away from him and I am lost in a world where my heart bleeds in loneliness.

With every move my soul feels like it's being ripped into pieces.

With every rip, I feel a little bit of me loses hope that we could overcome this. There were so many things that made me want to stay.

What would my life be like without him?

What is life without the security of another person loving you?

I can't think about the possibility that life without him could make me happy again.

Maybe it would remind me of what it means to smile again, laugh again, dream again.

Each morning I wake up hoping that this day will be better than the last. And by the grace of God and God alone it is. But the weight of uncertainty battles with my faith. I believe that I will get through it and I believe that it will work out for my good. But connecting the dots that all of this may happen without Joseph is something I just can't seem to fathom.

The thought of life without him makes the world I see grey with uncertainty.

SCENE THIRTEEN:
DEFEATED BY THE STORM

I was walking back home from the tube station one night after church. I remember it being colder than usual for a spring evening. I didn't drive to church that day because I went straight from work and when I left in the morning, I left without a jacket. The night breeze was so strong that evening, so I began to briskly walk home to escape the wind. As I continued on my commute home, I felt a vibration in my trouser pocket. It was my phone. I considered ignoring the call; picking up the phone would slow me down. Eventually I took out my phone to see it was him.

When I saw his name appear on the screen. I froze. I had only moments to decide what to do before the phone would stop ringing and go to voicemail. A gush of heat came running through me and the wind became still. I felt droplets of sweat roll down my forehead as the phone vibrated in my palm.

This was the moment I had been waiting for. I spent hours day in and day out longing for him to return my call. Each day I woke up hopeful that this was the day he would get in contact. My daily commute consisted of hopeful thoughts and my mind playing tricks on me. I lost count of the number of times I was stopped in my tracks by the whiff of what I thought was the smell of his cologne. My heart would grow giddy, only for me to realise that it wasn't him. But as one week became two and two weeks turned to three, the harsh reality was something I knew I could no longer hide from. The more time that passed, the more I came to terms with the possibility that he may never call me.

***

The phone continued to vibrate in my palms until I eventually picked it up. I had the phone pressed to my ear while I power walked home. I didn't know what he was going to say and I didn't want to be out on the street when he said it. I remember anticipation choking me as I answered his call, wondering what was coming. I didn't know what exactly would come but I knew it was something big. It had been 21 days since I heard his voice. 28 if I eliminate the 5 second conversation we had where he simply said he would call back, and never did.

Until now I still wonder why this call caught me by surprise. After three weeks of not hearing from him you would have thought that I knew what he would say. That I would have prepared myself for the possibility that this may be the end. But somewhere in me I believed that it was not the end. That maybe this was one of the many lessons he wanted to teach me. To be honest, like most of the 'lessons' he attempted to teach me in our relationship, I wasn't sure what I was supposed to learn, or even know what I had done to warrant a relationship that took on the form of a student teacher relationship. Why did every encounter start to feel like a classroom? But for some reason I remained his student because he was my favourite yet inexperienced, teacher that I'd become unhealthily familiar with.

When he began to speak, I realised that the call was not one of his classes where he would ask me if I had learnt my lesson, it was a call to tell me that this class was dismissed. Our relationship was over. I put my key through the front door quietly and tip toed upstairs to my room, hoping not to get my brother's attention, who I knew was home. By the time I got to my room, I was short of breath. The shortness in my breath was not because I hurried up the stairs, but because I had just heard the very thing I was dreading.

I immediately went into 'save this relationship at all cost' mode.

"Why?" I asked. "Surely, we haven't tried everything to save this relationship. Let's try counselling. Let us talk this through, speak to a pastor." In my frantic state, I offered endless suggestions, hoping he would agree to at least one.

I was willing to try anything but give up on us. After six years, and an eighteen month engagement, I refused to accept a phone call was sufficient to say it was over.

As I stood in my bedroom, the dreams I had that we could somehow overcome this came tumbling down and smashed right before me. In that moment, I came face to face with the truth: I had spent the last few years in a relationship that could never thrive even if somehow it managed to survive. I was being deflated day in and day out and I couldn't even see it. After six years of holding on, the storm had defeated us.

I no longer knew what it would feel like to do life without him.

I no longer wanted to know because I was afraid.

But with just one statement, I had to accept that everything was about to change.

When he hit me with those words, I finally asked the question I should have asked a long time ago: what kind of life would I have if we carried on? How would he have ever respected me as a woman if after neglecting me, leaving me to fix all the mess and treating what we had as a casual relationship, I stayed? Not only stayed but begged to stay.

But somewhere inside of me, I'd made myself believe that our relationship was worth the vulnerability of my pleas. At that moment, I couldn't see that God used him to do what I couldn't.

SCENE FOURTEEN:
TESTING OF MY FAITH

He attempted to end the relationship, but I wouldn't allow him to. I was holding on for dear life, so eventually, he humoured me by giving me an ultimatum.

As he stated the first condition and then went to the second and the third, I knew that it would take a miracle from God for this relationship to work. But I was determined for this miracle to happen. After all, God can move mountains, right? But the question for me wasn't if He could, but if He would.

One of the biggest errors I made was that I normalised the treatment in our relationship to be the standard. I was blindly holding on and calling it faith. I told myself over, and over, again that he was faithful and he respected my purity. These two things were so important to me that I missed out a key thing. Is this man one that will help me fulfil my destiny? The answer was cold no.

If I was unable to be the very best version of me in courtship with him, what made me think that marriage would change that? In my case, I became a shadow of the person I should have been when I was with him. All marriage would have done was enhance that.

n't need God to tell me something was wrong. But I kept ping. The only way I was going to walk away from this with head held high and with the knowledge that I tried everything I ould to make us succeed.

Today people ask me didn't I see the red flags. And in all honesty, to me there were no red flags. But the truth is I couldn't see these signs because the biggest red flag was me. I allowed myself to tolerate a life that I was not called to because I esteemed my feelings for Joseph over his character. I underestimated and undervalued the ever so beautiful and sacred institution I was about to enter. I chose wedding over marriage, desire over destiny and passion over purpose.

What I should have been doing was aligning my desire to my destiny and placing my passion in my purpose. But the more it became evident that Joseph was the odd piece to my puzzle, the more I kept attempting to remould the other pieces so that he could fit. And no matter how much I tried to even out those edges, or how close we got to fitting, there were always gaps. Gaps that he was never meant to fill.

The next day I called in sick to work. I had only been at this new job for 2 months and between a called off wedding and sick days, it was only God that favoured me to pass my probation. I knew I couldn't get through that day at work without breaking down. I kept replaying our conversation over and over again in my mind.

The ultimatums, which I will share as the book progresses, remained at the forefront of my mind. *How am I going to do this Lord?* I prayed to God, reminding him of just how powerful He is.

"If you could cause the red sea to part and the wall of Jericho to fall, surely you can do this too Lord!"

I was praying for God to change things to suit what I wanted when really, I needed Him to change me to see what I needed. With all this going on, I had to keep up the front that everything was okay. I didn't want my family to worry about me any more than they already were. I put on a brave face all through the painfully gruelling process. And it was not because I was fronting. But because somehow God kept me standing. But on this day, it didn't feel like the others. At any moment, I felt I could crumble.

That weekend was my friend's wedding. I had already given them my word that I would help them coordinate their big day and

I intended to stay faithful to it. I was not about to allow the misfortune of my relationship to cause me to be a bad friend to my loved ones.

As a result, I spent the day perfecting my poker face before proceeding to occupy myself with 101 things so I wouldn't have any time to think about the devastating conversation from the night before. Everything was going so well. I made it to the wedding and performed every task required of me and then some.

We'd made it to the end of the dinner and then it was time for the speeches. Each speech was so beautiful, but it was the groom's speech that defined things for me. As the groom spoke about his beautiful bride, I realised that there was once a time that Joseph spoke about me like that. I replayed the day he proposed to me repeatedly in my head. His speech was so heart-felt and everyone in that room could feel just how much he loved me and I him. I thought about the look in his eyes as he knelt there in the midst of friends and family.

"So many people dream of having someone who is God-fearing, beautiful, ambitious, smart, funny, creative and talented. I am so glad I am a part of the minority living this dream." These words from the night of the engagement stuck with me. How did we get from the couple on that day to the strangers we were today?

Driving home from the wedding is still a blur to me. I knew what needed to be done but accepting it was not something that I was ready to do. I didn't know if I had what it took to deal with the aftermath of a called off relationship. I didn't know if I was ready for the secrets, we had been keeping from our loved ones, to all be unveiled.

***

'My brethren count it all joy when you fall into various trials, knowing that the testings of your faith produces patience' James 1:2-8

9th May 2016

Waking up this morning was different. I did not follow my usual routine of quiet time with God and meditation followed by scrolling through my social media. Instead, I was still. My mind was so busy that I couldn't bring myself to start my day.

Up until now keeping my pain in was easier than letting people see the truth. No one could see what I didn't show them. As long as I looked like I was handling it, I would be fine. So, I kept it bottled in. I knew that if my true feelings came out, everything would change. But on this day, I was honest with myself that I no longer wanted to fight. I didn't want to keep the pain in any longer. I was tired of pretending that everything was okay.

On May 9th 2016, there were no more 'what if's'.

My insides could no longer withstand the aches of its brokenness. The uncertainty of my relationship had consumed me. I wasn't happy. I felt drained. I was in a relationship with someone who had made it clear to me that he did not want to be with me anymore. So, what on earth was I doing holding on after the pain of rejection, a broken heart and a wounded spirit?

I no longer had the will to fight. The battle in my mind was one that made me fear for my sanity. It did not just make me afraid but everyone around me.

To hear my father cry as he feared for my mental health and wellbeing was devastating. But to see the look in my mother's eyes, as she helplessly came to the realisation that this was a battle she couldn't fight for me, is a sight engraved in my memory. My parents had spent all of my life protecting me. Little did they know that the greatest protection I needed was from the one who they intended to give me away to. Each day I fought multiple battles. The battle to hide my pain, the battle to protect my relationship and the battle to keep on smiling so my parents would stop blaming themselves for a mistake that I made.

Eventually I had no more fight. The will to stop pretending was outweighed by the will to face the consequences of hiding behind the scenes. This was a will that came through the never-ending strength of God.

Eventually, I picked myself out of bed, fell to my knees and prayed.

I could not control the quivering in my knees or the escalated pace of each breath as I started to speak. It was almost like my spirit knew the battles to come and that this decision was one that my life depended on. Deep down I knew the words to say but did not have the power to say them. Somewhere between waking up that morning and getting ready to face yet another day, my body lost the ability to hold it together. With my body curled up and eyes shut closed, I ignored the formulated words entangled in sophisticated sentences. Instead I said the words concealed in my heart. As I closed my eyes and let the moments continue to pass, my heart spoke, "Lord I do not want to *struggle* for this anymore."

In that moment, I felt free. Almost like God was waiting for me to let go so HE could give me some form of peace. It felt good. Scary, but good. Are you telling me that the beginning of my freedom was really contained in those nine words? I lifted my body up from its foetus position and knelt down.

A few moments later I raised my head. There was no debating this one. It was time to let Joseph go.

With each passing day, the signs were there to show me that God had truly delivered me from something. But my desire to stay in this toxic relationship was so high that my emotions towards the last few days were speaking louder than that ever so gentle voice inside of me called the Holy Spirit. I knew the sacrifices that I had made for this relationship to work and for us to be together. I knew that ending this was more than just going our separate ways.

It's easy to admit now that it was pride that kept me holding on for so long. I miscalculated the importance of saving face instead of saving destiny. I was willing to throw elements of my life and happiness away because I was more concerned about the 6 years I had committed to this relationship. But what was six years compared to eternity? I had my whole life ahead of me and I wanted to spend it with the one who will live each day with me building for both sides of eternity.

I got ready for the day and made my way to work. Walking up the stairs of the underground station, I realised that I put my engagement ring on that morning. A ring that symbolised a commitment that was now broken. Without hesitation, I took it off.

When I took off the ring and put it in my purse, I looked down at my bare finger and I caught myself smiling. I found myself smiling through the foreign feeling of taking off a band that I had worn every day for the last nineteen months.

I looked at the tan lines from where my ring use to be. I knew that this reminder was one that could trigger me. So I laid my hands on my finger and I prayed that God would remove every reminder of this ring trace. I opened up my eyes and like magic, the tan lines were no longer there. I knew it was not magic, it was an instant miracle from God.

If I had any doubts that this was the end before, this made it very clear.

Now I see that the very thing I was afraid of, I was already doing. I was scared to do life without Joseph but truthfully, I had already been doing life without him. Heartbreak had me believing a list of impossibilities instead of focussing on the possibilities that were right in front of me. Possibilities I was living.

I spent 21 days waiting for hear from him. In those 21 days, I was strengthened beyond belief, but the state of my emotions meant that even though I knew God had been with me, all I could think of was how my life would be without him. There was a hidden treasure attached to the heart ache of those 21 days. I felt the unfailing love of God at the very same time I felt the failing love of man. I was able to put the confidence I once put in man, in God.

When I got into the office, I made my way to a private room and I picked up the phone and made the courageous step. I told him that it was the end and that I accepted it.

I came to the realisation long before this moment that being with someone who doesn't want to be with you leads to a life of misery. It didn't immediately dawn on me then just how much we were both risking by staying in this relationship. If I realised then, maybe I wouldn't have eluded to the fact that my decision was purely based on what he said to me when I called him to break things off. Maybe I would have boldly told him that I don't want to spend another moment with him when there are so many great moments ahead that are depending on me to be the person I am supposed to be.

Nonetheless, I told him what he wanted to hear. And he and I were both free. A little bit of me wondered whether he really meant it when he told me that he didn't think we should be together. And that is why his response never surprised me. I was finally giving him the exit he wanted. But when I spoke to him, there was a sense of confusion and denial in his voice.

I could feel myself getting angry as he breathed ever so erratically over the phone. I waited a moment, hoping he would say something back that would indicate that I was making this entire scenario up in my head. He didn't.

Before I could take back my words, I hung up and did not look back. For me this was the end of my relationship. The end of a six year chapter. But I knew all too well that this was not the end but instead, it was the beginning.

SCENE FIFTEEN:
SECRETS UNVEILED

Dear Friend,
So, I had to take out this moment in the book to address you.
God willing, thousands and maybe millions of people may read this book.
To them they will experience my life vicariously. But for you, you experienced it
right beside me.
You stood by me and supported me through the storm. And I thank you.
What I am about to say will come to you as a shock.
This information being withheld is not because I didn't trust you or because
I didn't at times want to tell you.
I never thought it would come to this point. The point that my relationship
would fail and that the decisions I made would come back to haunt me.
For you, the day I told you the relationship was over was the end of this
chapter. But for me it was the opening of a new one.
For the next 25 months I faced a battle I didn't think I would ever have to
fight. One that involved lawyers, many tears and undeniable strength. It was a
battle that not only cost me financially but almost cost me my health.
The day the relationship ended, I was not only ending an engagement, but a
marriage. If I am honest, I didn't think I would get to this point. The point
where I would be in my mid-20's and have to go through this. As if a called off
wedding was not enough! Now a called of marriage?
At the time of writing this letter, I am halfway through a legal battle with
a man I once loved. If you are reading this letter, then that means I have come
out on the other side of this.

But for some reason the fear of sharing this with you was so much harder than the fear of going through the process.

I am sorry for not being the transparent Sarah you once knew. I am sorry that years have passed and I could still not summon the courage to tell you face to face.

As you turn the pages of this book, I hope you can understand my story a bit better. The mood swings, the random outbursts and the seasons when I ran away.

My dear loved ones, I am sorry.

Love,

Sarah.

PART 4

SCENE SIXTEEN: DECISIONS

The waiting game was one that I'd thought I became familiar with. The 21 days I waited to hear back from Joseph were the hardest 21 days of my life. But I would soon learn that harder days were to come.

As the days turned into weeks, the weeks into months and the months into years, my life as I knew it would change in a way that no one could have ever prepared me for. I never knew anyone who had ended a marriage at least not personally. Everything, including my faith, was challenged and this season required me to trust the unseen like never before.

In the midst of getting over a failed relationship I was being presented with options on how to end a marriage. Never in my wildest dreams did I imagine that this would happen to me. I went back and forth on all the reasons why this should not have been my story. After all, I did everything the way I was told to. I have never been one to look back and blame God, but I will be the first person to admit that this situation tested my faith. It was only a few years prior that I rolled my eyes at the fact that a certain reality celebrity was married for all of 72 days. How I wish I could take that back.

At such a young age, I was faced with what quickly became emotional torture. When I accepted that ring, I committed to being in this for the long haul. I just wish that when I took those vows, I thought about what the 'long haul' could potentially look like.

I signed on the dotted line thinking less highly of the significance it carried. I saw it as a part of the process but not the solidifying of it. You see, growing up in the Christian faith meant that I placed more value on the church blessing than I did the legal one. But I soon learnt that the one that could be upheld in the eyes of the law, was the one that breaking would lead me into lawyer talks, court hearings and emotional trauma.

Explaining this part of my journey is something that I have dreaded for the last two years.

I wondered how people would view me if they knew that I was legally married. Two people, both of Christian faith and both ending a marriage that arguably never really started. How do you adequately describe making a lifetime commitment that would only see the lifetime of the average cockroach? How do I tell my friends and family that I married someone who would one day turn around and ask me to walk away from it? Was my sense of judgment really that bad?

When we made the decision to get legally married, it seemed smart. But I have learnt that what seems smart, isn't always wise.

Joseph and I decided to live in England over me relocating to Nigeria. It was what made sense. For starters, it was the only country that we both lived in and the country where we wanted to build together. We knew that this was not going to be an easy challenge. Joseph is a Nigerian Citizen who lived in the UK during his studies. I, on the other hand, had lived in the UK all my life. With the changes to government policy, it would have been easier for me to relocate to my motherland than it would have been for Joseph to stay. We knew even before we got engaged that the process would be a hard one. I also knew that if it had not been for me, Joseph would have gladly continued his life in Nigeria. But he met me and for this reason, and so much more, him moving to England was the only option we were both fully committed to.

If that commitment meant that I was going to forfeit my dreams of a perfect wedding experience, then I would. And I did. The toil that the distance placed on our relationship is what led us to this decision.

February 2015, I'd made a career transition which meant I had to go through probation on a new role and in a new company. It had been 5 months since we had seen each other. Things had not quite turned out the way we expected when Joseph moved away. I didn't expect to be starting a new job and he did not expect to still be looking for one. The strain on our relationship was so intense it was hard to articulate; words did not do it justice. Days would go pass and I felt as if I was walking on eggshells. Joseph has always been a man with a plan and naturally, he desired to be a provider. The fact that he was unable to do the things he planned to do was hard for him. Having to carry the weight on his shoulders of not being able to prepare for our future financially due to being unemployed was a weight that was far too heavy for him to carry.

***

March 2015

I finally passed my probation at work, but I was not given the clearance to travel until after the General Elections. It was a big time in UK politics, and it was so great that I got the opportunity to be one of the people working on a major political campaign. It was a dream that I always had but with everything going on I wished the Elections would either take a back seat or come sooner.

I remember calling our family to let them know that I had to wait to travel and it was one phone call that changed everything. It was the phone call that presented me with a proposal that I thought could stop all of our problems.

My mum and Joseph's mum were together in Lagos when I called. They had grown to build a beautiful relationship through the time of our courtship that blossomed once we were engaged. Because of this, my mum made it a point to always make time to visit Joseph's parents whenever she visited Lagos.

I tried to reach Joseph first but surprise, surprise; there was no answer. I knew our mums were together, so I gave them a call to let them know I had passed my probation at work. I was on loudspeaker so I could hear that they were both so pleased for me. But this feeling soon dwindled as soon as I told them that I had to wait a few months before I could travel to visit Joseph in Lagos.

The western side of me wanted to say, "if you are sad then how about me?". But of course, they are Nigerian so the Nigerian girl in me was reminded that such expressions of emotions are not typically expressed to your elders, let alone your parents.

Joseph's mum quickly took the phone and began to speak.

"Hello, my Angel." Joseph's mum and I were so close. 'Angel' was one of the many pet names she addressed me by throughout the years.

"I am worried about Joseph." she said.

My heart began to drop. I knew that Joseph had been off with me and so it should have been obvious to me that the ones he lived with were also experiencing his change of moods.

She told me that her son hadn't been the same. He was no longer the bubbly, accommodating Joseph everyone knew and loved.

"So, what do we do, mum?" I asked my soon to be mother in law.

She replied, "After a conversation with your mum, we both think that the two of you should go to the registry and get married."

Shocked by what I had just heard, I took a slight pause before I eventually asked, "Why? Are you suggesting we move the wedding forward?"

"No." She responded. "If you go to the registry, you can apply for a spousal visa for Joseph. Once you have been in this job for 6 months, you will be able to put the application through and Joseph can move to London before the church wedding and start his life there."

They have really thought this through, I thought to myself.

This was the very last thing I expected to hear when I gave the mums a call that afternoon.

Everything felt so heavy and I knew that ultimately this was a decision that only myself and Joseph could make. But my response in this moment would determine whether we proposed the idea to Joseph or not.

I can still remember the pace of my heart escalating. I had no one to turn to for advice. How do I even begin to explain the 'whys' as they come in.

Both of our mothers expected an immediate answer from me. I was surprised as to how and why my mum wouldn't at least give me the heads up that this was coming. Maybe she was equally as shocked as I was, or maybe she thought it was a great Idea.

"So, if we get legally married, would I be addressed as his wife?" I naively asked.

"Technically yes, but culturally no. Culturally until your traditional wedding, you aren't married." Joseph's mum replied. "And since you have both decided not to consummate your marriage until your church blessing, then really you aren't married until your church blessing."

This is all I needed to hear to at least consider it. I wanted the day the world knew I was his wife to be a special day that happened in the presence of our family and friends. Not a day in a registry office with only a few of the people we love.

Without further hesitation, I agreed to think about it. And I guess they took that as a yes because a few hours later my phone began to ring. It was Joseph. His mum had told him about our conversation and as I predicted, he was not keen on the idea. Doing this would mean that we would be married for almost a year before we do our church blessing.

I knew that if we did this, it would be because of me. Joseph wanted us to do things the right way. Traditional then the church blessing and registry all in one. That way there were no blurred lines of our roles.

We toiled with the idea for a few days.

I thought of every possible reason why this would be the best thing for us to do. All I wanted was for Joseph and I to be okay. And if that meant speeding up the process for him to come back to the UK, the place where he was never supposed to leave, then maybe this was the right thing to do.

I shared my thoughts with Joseph, but he still was not keen on the idea.

"What would we tell our friends?" he asked

"We don't." I replied sharply.

"Babes, we are getting married anyway so they will never have to know."

I knew he asked me this question because he never wanted anyone to ever question his motives for marrying me. Him having a visa was not the reason why Joseph wanted to marry me. I knew that, he knew that and so did everyone around us. But with so much stigma being attached to African men marrying for 'papers' I knew without him saying it that he did not want to put me or him through that scrutiny. Truthfully, I know he was more worried about what it would do to me. He was not one to really care about public opinion. I on the other hand was.

I reassured him that everything would be ok and eventually I managed to convince Joseph to reluctantly agree.

A few weeks later, I purchased a white dress off the high street and flew to Lagos.

At the time, it didn't feel right. Our siblings were not there or aware that we were about to take this step. I knew if I told my brothers they would ask me to think about it rationally. To take away culture and to take away religion and think. Once I signed on that dotted line, we were married. I knew I didn't want to hear it, so I never told them.

Although it didn't feel right, it felt necessary.

We had the registry in the Summer of 2015. Surrounded only by our parents, a few friends who lived in Lagos whom we eventually told, but swore them to secrecy, and the registrar.

It took me a while to accept it, but I should have never pushed Joseph. Whether our mothers wanted this for us or not, I knew that if I pulled the plug, Joseph would have gladly pulled the plug too.

I was so sure that this was the only way for us to have a normal relationship. The thought of us having a long distance marriage was a nightmare that I did not want to live, so without thinking about the possibility that the problems we were already facing could multiply, we went ahead.

After the registry, we maintained our decision to abstain from sex until our church blessing. This was important for me. By doing this, it meant that I could push the registry to the back of my mind. It would be a formality. It wouldn't be the date of the anniversary we would mark, or even a date we spoke about. It was a formality.

Even after the traditional, I decided that if we waited this long, we may as well continue to wait. This was not always a joint decision and at some points it was very much a decision that I wish I never made. It was hard.

I mean let's be honest, I was sexually attracted to Joseph as he was to me. But my conviction to wait was far more important to me. Some may say, we were licenced to have sex. A registry and a traditional. But from the moment we were engaged, we decided to wait until after the church blessing. This was way before any talk of a registry came into play. It was a conviction that I refused to ignore and one I chose to honour before God.

Sometimes we make decision that we will never understand. But God knew that It was a decision that would help me get through this process. Emotionally, spiritually and legally. By not having sex, I could end this marriage without going through the dreaded 'D' word. Don't get me wrong, I know divorce is a part of life. I just didn't want it to be a part of mine. When I was informed that the marriage met the grounds of annulment, there was a sigh of relief. It didn't at all make the situation okay, but it did make it easier for me to come to grips with.

We could annul the marriage as if it never even happened. Sounds straightforward, right? Well think again. The battle I was due to enter, no one could prepare me for. In the twinkle of an eye, the person who I believed was destined to be my biggest ally, became my biggest enemy. Things became ugly and fast.

SCENE SEVENTEEN:
25 MONTHS

So now I have told you this, I can tell you what the conditions were when he called me to discuss the future of our relationship.

Ultimatum 1: We must get an annulment
Ultimatum 2: You have to move to Nigeria
Ultimatum 3: Our parents need to get along

I wish I could sugar coat these ultimatums more than I already have. As he relayed the terms, he set for our relationship to continue, I wondered who on earth I entered a legally binding contract with. Because this man on the other side of the phone, was not the man I knew. No way would I commit to the most important decision in my life to date with someone who had the capability of turning around and ending it without exploring every option first.

It quickly dawned on me that there was a way he could. I knew long before this moment that in a battle of resilience, Joseph couldn't even take the heat. In the years we were together, I saw him run from situations and not fight for what mattered to him. Why did I expect to be any different? I was under the illusion that with marriage, it will be different. But it wasn't. The very issues I ignored were amplified. And it would soon cost me the very thing I thought I wanted the most. This relationship.

When he called me that day, he already knew what he wanted to do. When he told me that he had already spoken to a lawyer, my heart shattered.

"I have the papers." He said. "All you have got to do is agree to these ultimatums and sign it if you agree. Or sign it if you don't agree." Either way, he wanted this annulment to happen.

It hurt so much to think that in the 21 days I spent waiting for him to call me back, he was out there instructing a lawyer to annul our marriage.

I couldn't call my friends because the vast majority of them did not know we were legally married. I couldn't call my family because their loyalties to me would mean that they would have given me impartial advice. I called my Bishop. I needed whatever action I took in that moment to be informed by wisdom. I was too emotional to hear from God in that moment.

I remember calling by Bishop in tears. Crying about this decision that I had to make. I mean what was the point of trying to work things out when once again, he was willing to break a commitment with me? Would I waste even more time trying to fix a relationship with a man who had repeatedly shown me that he is not committed enough to try?

I had spent years committing to making us work and in just moments, he was tearing it all down. Of course, I cannot speak on what it took for him to get to this point. The point where I would be hit with the request to end our marriage. But all I knew is somewhere between the thought and the action, he should have spoken to me. My Bishop knew that ultimately, I had to make the decision. But the words he said to me that day were filled with clarity. The words of a man who loved us both and wanted to see us both win. In this case, the winning was not what I thought it was only a few weeks prior. Then, I thought winning would be us getting through this and making our relationship work.

Eventually it became clear that staying with a person who was willing to give everything up at the stench of adversity is not winning. It is losing. My Bishop had seen me cry, seen me pray, seen me fight so hard for this to work. He contended with me and for me.

In his softly spoken voice, he said to me exactly what my spirit needed to hear. "Sarah, if that is what he wants to do, you can't force his hand to stay."

Even with this truth, I still didn't want us to end. "But what about the marriage Bishop?" I cried. "This isn't God's will for me." I said in a queering tone.

After allowing me cry and vent, he responded, "You are not the one who is breaking this relationship. You are not the one who is walking away. Sarah, you can't keep chasing someone who is not ready."

When he said these words, 'It resonated with something deep inside of me. It was the first time someone told me exactly how it was. I had been chasing a man who was not ready.

I continued to weep over the phone.

"He can't do this, Bishop." I replied. "He can't."

After I calmed down, my Bishop prayed for me and after he prayed, he said

"Sarah, let him proceed with the annulment. God will see you both through."

At first, I didn't want to heed to his advice. I wanted to stay and fight. But eventually, every word he said to me sank in and I couldn't ignore them. The weekend passed and again, I couldn't ignore the further confirmation at my friend's wedding. The love and happiness I witnessed on this day was enough for me to know that I wanted more for myself.

So I decided that I would agree to the annulment.

I really struggled to understand why he even gave me the ultimatums. Why there was a choice in it for me when it was clear that he didn't think about me when he made the decision to call it quits.

But I knew the reason he gave me a choice had nothing to do with me. It was all to do with him. He didn't want to wake up one day and realise that he had made a mistake. At least if he left the ball in my court, it would be my fault. It didn't matter that the ball was deflated and pierced across the surface when he gave it to me. All that mattered is that someone other than him made a lifelong decision on his behalf.

These were trends I saw in our relationship that I ignored. At the time, I didn't realise I was doing both him, and myself, a disservice by ignoring these traits. I noticed early on that when it came to the important decisions in his life, he would look to someone close to him to help him make them. Initially, I thought it was cute when he would ask for my input on important life choices. I felt honoured that right from an early stage in our relationship he displayed these traits. It was not until one of the decisions we made together went south that I realised his conscious decision to involve me was really a way for him to find someone to blame should it all go wrong. It was something I overlooked in the hope that it would get better.

It took professional counselling for me to realise that one of my biggest flaws in this relationship was trying to be his everything. In my desire to be needed, instead of wanted, I stayed with a man who couldn't make his own decisions.

In the words of one of my dear pastors turned sister, Reverend Ayo, "Some women think they are Bob the Builder. We try to build a relationship and along the way try to fix our men when we see things that we don't like or change the things that only God can change."

For a while, I told myself that I let everyone down.

There were so many people rooting for us to work, there were friends who had sacrificed so much. Not just financially but emotionally. And there was no way I could ever repay them. And I don't mean a financial repayment. No. I mean how do you repay back time or the hope they lost in our relationship working.

And then there was my family. Oh, my precious family. They had put so much into making me happy.

The look on my dad's face when he saw me broken and the sound of my mum tears are memories that I will never forget. Images that haunted me for months as I closed my eyes and attempted to forget about the events that will soon become 'old news'.

With everything I felt, there were some days that all it took was the pain of an aching parent to give me the motivation I needed to ensure that they would never ache for me like this again.

In my pain all I could do was think about getting strong; strong for them. So, they can see that their little girl was not broken but only waiting to be restored.

They spent years investing into me and for what? A failed love to break down the pieces that it took them years to build. God forbid, this could not be my testimony. I refused. All the feeling of self-doubt, worthlessness, bitterness and hurt were so evident; I made a decision that these feelings were only temporary lodgers squatting in a residence that did not belong to them.

I worked so hard to prepare myself for the makeover that I knew God was giving to me. I don't mean the physical makeover, but the makeover that removed the fear of living, and stripped away this new reality of brokenness.

I knew that getting strong was not just for my parents. Neither was it for my friends who have only ever known me as the strong one. It was for me too.

The journey was not a short one, but it was a driven one. Driven with purpose to overcome. There were no fancy accolades to my mission. It was a mission that required me to submit my heart, mind and body to God.

It was a decision that I made before the depression kicked in, before I began to suffer from anxiety and developed a sleep disorder. I say this because even when the obstacles appeared along the way, they did not distract me from my mission.

I had to have faith that this treacherous walk to overcoming would finally bear great fruit. But I had to know where I was going to in order for me to never give up along the way.

To many, I was strong, and they were right. My weakness is made perfect in God's strength and boy, oh boy, was I weak. But it was strength that God gave that allowed me to face every day even when things got difficult.

It was the community around me that knew the full story that kept me.

The days Pastor Ayo would call me just to affirm me and remind me I was more than this. The nights Kara would pray on the phone with me when anxiety robbed me of sleep.

I was 25 and going through an annulment. I had so many years ahead of me but there were moments when this felt like a death sentence; on those days, I was blessed for the sweet comfort of God that He gave me through His children.

I hoped that as the days went on, everything would get easier. But when sleep deprivation kicked in, my days felt like they were never ending. And for the next 18 months of my life, the days seemed to get harder and harder and the only bit of light shining through was that of the confidence I held in God.

SCENE EIGHTEEN:
EVERYONE NEEDS A POOL

A few days after my conversation with Joseph, I received an email from him detailing the stages his lawyer had taken for the annulment. I was prepared for this email to come but nothing could truly prepare me for how it would feel when it actually came. I didn't know anyone who had been through an annulment before. I mean, as much as I watched Keeping Up with the Kardashians in its formative years, I did not actually know the Kardashian family, nor did I have any access to ask Kim K how she got through an annulment.

I had no physical person to guide me through it. I soon learnt that this was the biggest blessing. I have no doubt that God knew that I needed to have no one with this experience guiding me. If I did then maybe I would have been even more disappointed at how lengthy mine was compared to the average couple. Going through this with God as my guide meant I held on to Him like my life depended on it. And truly I did.

I didn't have time to feel sorry for myself or even process what was happening. All I could think of was the moment it would finally be over. The moment that I would no longer have this hanging over my head day to day. It was bad enough that I would go to sleep, and my dreams consisted of what was, and broken memories. Or even that I was confronted with what felt like a massive stain every time the stares of pity came from people who knew me, and those who heard about the wedding being called off. I could ignore these things. But to have to deal with lawyers and paperwork in the midst of it were things I could not ignore.

The stage of processing the annulment was by no means expected to be easy, but I didn't anticipate just how hard it would be.

Weeks had passed and I began to realise that everything had gone quiet. I went from finding out the next steps of the annulment process, to being kept out of the loop completely. I did all I could to avoid contact with Joseph. I had to protect my peace of mind and my heart. But when things changed and all I had was radio silence, I made the decision to get in contact with him.

I sent him an email asking him for an update. Days passed before I would eventually get a response. I could not help but grow increasingly anxious. My life was in limbo and the person who seemed to be holding all of the cards was not being forthcoming.

When he finally responded to my email, the reply gave me no confidence that this process would be a smooth one.

It had been two months since the annulment had been filed. Two months I spent trying to piece together a puzzle that never fully had all of its pieces in the first place. Eventually I knew I had to stop before I drove myself crazy. I was drowning in a pool of self pity and trying to make sense of it kept me trapped in this relationship that was no more.

So, I decided to do something for me. Something not relationship or marriage related. Something to keep my head above the water. I decided that it was time for me to learn how to swim. And I don't mean figuratively, I mean I literally went online and enrolled to swimming lessons.

This was exactly what I needed. I spent the last few months feeling like all I was doing was losing. I needed something for me. Something that would be a win. Something I could look back at and say, "I am glad I did that!". I may have felt like I was taking many L's in 2016 but at least I finally learnt how to swim!

Swimming soon became my safe haven. Every week on a Wednesday evening at 7pm, I would step into that pool and it would be me and the water. As my face hit the water, everything above ground felt far away. With every stroke pushing away from the resistance, I was one step closer to the finishing line. The pool was what I needed. No one knew me in these lessons. When they saw me, I wasn't Sarah the girl with a broken relationship, I was just Sarah. The girl in the beginners swimming class who was too afraid to let her feet off the ground. I was the girl who made everyone laugh whenever she would randomly scream five seconds after I finally trusted my body to allow me to float. In the pool, there was no baggage. The pool taught me how to use everything I had within me to survive. As long as I kept moving, I was not going to drown.

I knew that this was true for my life outside of the pool too. As long as I kept using every word of God I had stored in me to combat what I was seeing, I could win this. My faith could overcome this.

So I kept at it and every time I wanted to give up, I remembered the pool.

***

It was a Wednesday afternoon. I was at my work desk getting ready to leave for my swimming lesson when an email came in from Joseph. Nervous about what this email would entail, I hesitated before I eventually summoned the courage to open it.

To my surprise, he emailed me to ask me if he could call me that evening. I called Kara. She was one of the few people who were aware of the annulment. I told her about the email, and she said, "Maybe he has an update from the courts."

But something inside of me knew that his intentions for calling had nothing to do with the annulment.

I reluctantly emailed back giving him the go ahead to get in contact after my lesson. I remember walking back home from the leisure centre when I saw his missed call. I battled with myself as to whether I should call him back or wait for him to call me. I walked about 50 yards before I finally gave in and dialled his number.

"Hi Sarah." He said.

On the other side of the phone wasn't the cold man who broke up with me only two months prior. It was the man I met six years ago. I could feel my heart soften by the sound of his voice.

What did this mean? We are in what I thought was mid annulment settlement and officially over. But this had been the first time I had heard the guy I knew speak in so long that I felt weak.

For a moment there was silence on the phone. I needed to gather my thoughts and snap out of this moment.

He didn't wait for me to return the greeting.

"I know I don't deserve to ask you this, or even deserve to know the answer to this question. But I just want to ask you how you are?"

And as if there was ever a moment to snap out of it, there it was.

How I am? Seriously? How do you think I am?

Of course, this is not what I said, even though I really wanted to. Instead I responded with what any true Nigerian would respond. "I am doing great, thank you. Just getting back from swimming lessons."

I wanted him to know that my life did not all of a sudden go on pause with his exit.

As the conversation continued, I could sense that he missed me. I began to think that maybe he wanted to know if I missed him too. He spoke to me almost as if nothing had happened. And honestly, so did I. The walk home was about 20 minutes and for the whole time we spoke about everything from his job to mine and even my swimming lessons.

It was not until I arrived at the end of my road that it dawned on me that I was giving him what he wanted. My presence. He didn't deserve my presence.

Not once was the annulment mentioned in that conversation or the fact that I still had not forgiven him for how he treated me. Instead he asked how I was and then gave me a mini run down on all the new events in his life.

I hated that I still loved him and the more he spoke, the more I realised that as much as he had hurt me, that love was still there.

I quickly told him that I had to go. I didn't know what this call meant but I knew after that call that more than ever, I had to guard myself. I couldn't put myself in the position where my healing heart would be compromised.

Other than processing the annulment, we had no reason to talk to one another.

***

Four months after the filing, I heard nothing. With every email requesting information came an excuse as to why I had not yet received the papers. I went from wanting to save this relationship to wanting it to end. The weight of knowing that I was still legally married to this man was an enormous weight that no one could carry for me. Although my family and friends who knew tried, it was not their cross to carry.

There were days that I wanted to believe that the excuses were true. But how could I trust a man who could do this to me.

Eventually I picked up the phone and called him.

"Joseph, what is happening with the annulment and why haven't I received the papers?" In the middle of being taken back by my reaction, he said the three words I had given up on. He told me he was sorry. Not sorry for the delay in the annulment but sorry for everything leading up to it.

Immediately, I began to cry. I couldn't decipher if it was tears of finally receiving an apology or if it was purely because I never expected him to take any form of ownership for the pain he'd caused me.

He told me he was sorry, told me he had been thinking on how he could get to me, show me he was sorry and how much he missed me.

"21 days." I cried. "21 days is how long you said it took you to realise you could cope living without me."

"Well, I am not coping." He admitted

"You called me a habit." I exclaimed, my voice dripping with hurt as tears cascaded down my face

"I am sorry, Sarah." He said.

After a few minutes, I realised that the lump developed in my throat was not because I was at a loss for words, but because there was something about this apology that gave me a sense of discomfort.

This is what I thought I wanted two months ago but being faced with the reality of it, I realised that there was no apology in the world that would take me back to the girl who would love him to her detriment.

I knew that, but did he?

I had always been at the other end of his apologies with arms opened wide to take him back and pick up where we left off.

But not this time.

This time I knew that my worth was far more than three words that would soon be preceded with the same relationship we once had. It was not that I believed Joseph was a bad man or incapable of being a good partner. I just knew that with all of our history, with all of the signs I saw and ignored and with the pain I was still feeling, there was no way that I would have been able to trust him the way a partner should be trusted.

Most importantly, I couldn't see a life where we fulfilled purpose and thrived together.

I knew that no matter what he said, I would remain unmoveable, and I did. Through the attempts to make amends and the apologies, I was unmoveable. In the process, he admitted delaying the annulment in the hope that we could work it out. But after hearing that I was through, he knew that he had to proceed.

I still loved him, and I knew that he knew that too. We hear so many sayings about love, one being that love isn't enough. But one day it challenged me; was it that love was not enough or that *our* love wasn't enough?

God loved us so much that He gave us His son. That love was and still is enough. If we are made in the image and likeness of God, why isn't love enough?

But you see, that love came with action.

The reason why love was not enough for us was because the love I was experiencing, and in some respects, the love I was giving him, didn't always understand sacrifice. Love should encompass all the things that make up a fruitful and healthy relationship. It should be patient and kind. Not jealous or boastful, proud or rude. It shouldn't demand its own way or be irritable. It should not keep records of wrongdoing or rejoice in injustice. Love never gives up, it never loses faith, is always hopeful and endures through every circumstance.

So many times I felt that my relationship was held for as long as it was because I loved him and he loved me. When we started, I could honestly say we were like best friends. But as time progressed and wounds were left unhealed, we stopped being patient with one another. Time after time, we used our wrongs against one another. And eventually his "love" gave up.

For those weeks that I never heard from him after the wedding was postponed, I remained hopeful that someday we would work this out. I held on to the faith because love endures.

But he no longer had faith in our relationship and, although at the time I was crushed by it, I now look back and realise how thankful I should be.

I was willing to endure what stopped being 'God's kind of love' without even realising it.

By the end of the call, I knew that Joseph would do all he could to slow down the annulment process, and I was right.

This was the genesis of delay tactics that made what should have been a six months process take over two years.

There are so many parts of the annulment timeline that I pushed to the back of my memory. The trauma of it meant that at the time we were going through it, archiving it was better than dealing with it. I didn't have time to dwell on the trust broken or the monster this created in him.

The ugliness of the months to follow consisted of false promises, inconsistent stories and the blame shift game.

Months of being promised a delivery in the post only to never receive it. It was always the fault of FedEx or DHL.

My better judgment believed him the first two times I chased him for the papers. But eventually, I had to see it for what it was. A tactic. Countless times I would ask for the tracking number of these papers. To which there was never one provided.

I got tired of the back and forth.

Each time we spoke I became more and more deflated. I was still in the process of healing from our breakup but every time I was confronted with disappointment from yet another delay in the process, it took me a few steps backwards.

He pushed for this annulment and I fought to stop it. It took tears and counsel to get me to the point where I was willing to let go. Even when I let go, there was still something in me that wanted to fight. But after months of going through counselling and understanding my self-worth, I finally accepted that this was for the best. Him now trying to put a spanner in the works was a slap in the face. I didn't want to have ill thoughts towards him or allow bitterness to invade my heart, but it did.

I knew I could not go on being bounced about like a yoyo from one story to another.

Joseph filed in Nigeria which meant that there was literally no way for me to track the process. It was now approaching nine months since he filed and still there was nothing.

Eventually the perfect opportunity presented itself for me to check on things. Our mutual friend was getting married in Nigeria. This would be my first time back since everything happened. Although I was nervous at the prospects of seeing him, I let him know I was planning on coming.

Since the postal system was apparently the reason why I had not received the documents, he now had the opportunity to present it to me in person. Weeks ahead of my arrival, I informed him I would be in town so that the papers could be served.

Despite the back and forth and my suspicion of his dishonesty, I figured that since the ball was in his court, I needed to remain amicable.

He assured me that the paperwork will be sorted, and I had nothing to worry about.

A few weeks before my arrival to Lagos, I sent him a message reminding him of my visit. And again, I was promised that all was in order.

For obvious reasons, I had my doubts that this was true but all I had was his word; so, I held on to it.

The day I landed in Lagos was a memorable day for many reasons. I had messages of encouragement from my friends who knew that the wedding would be the first time I would have seen Joseph since the break-up. Of course, the vast majority of my friends did not know that I was going through this annulment process so to them seeing Joseph was my biggest anxiety. But really, my biggest worry was that I would leave Nigeria the same way I came; with unsigned annulment papers.

The morning I landed, I drove to my cousin's house where I would stay for the duration of my stay, got a few hours sleep and had to get up and ready to make my way to my friend's bridal shower. She had no idea I would arrive on time for the shower. When I waked though the gates and she saw me, she ran and gave me a hug and of course in true 21st century style she shared this moment on social media with the caption 'Look who is in town!'

It was only a matter of time before Joseph saw this.

I never told Joseph my exact date of arrival. Instead I gave him a window of when I will be available. I didn't want anything to take away from this weekend. I wanted to celebrate my friend, have a good time with the girls and deal with the legalities of our relationship after the weekend.

Part one of the bridal shower was over and it was now time to head to part 2 of the hen festivities.

I got into the car and just as I pulled out of the driveway, a message came through on my phone. It was Joseph.

I had no expectations of what the message would read. I assumed that maybe he had seen I was here and was reaching out. At first, I put my phone back in my bag with little intention to open the message.

But of course, curiosity got the best of me.

'Hey Sarah, I have just seen that you have arrived! Welcome! I have been so sick these past few days that I forgot you were coming.'

When I saw the message, I already knew that an excuse would follow. I decided not to respond immediately and focus on enjoying the night.

As hard as I tried to put the message behind me, I couldn't help but think about it.

The next day, I received a call from Joseph. He began with the usual pleasantries before hitting me with the bombshell I had suspected.

"Sarah, I am really sorry, but I don't think the papers will be ready on time."

At this point I was raging. "What do you mean?" I angrily replied. "How can it not be ready Joseph?"

I could feel tears starting to form and with everything in me, I held them back. He did not deserve my tears.

With a bout of confidence that I didn't know I had, I said "It has been nine months since you filed, eight months since you sent me the draft filing via email, seven months since you said I would get the approved copy in the post, six months since you allegedly posted it, five months since you came clean with the fact that you were intentionally delaying the annulment, four months since you apparently sent me the papers, three months since I stopped believing a word that came out of your mouth, two months since your lawyer stopped answering my lawyers calls and one month since you have known that I would be coming to town. Nine months, Joseph. Nine months."

For nine months it felt like he had my life in his hands. But unlike a woman carrying life, these nine months did not end with a delivery.

I had no control or power over what was happening to me and I hated it.

There were strings attached to my back and, like a puppet, he pulled at them whenever he pleased. I was backed into a corner. I couldn't do anything other than wait for him to decide it was time to move on.

From the wedding being called off, to our breakup, to this annulment; I had no say in the matter.

I was tired.

I called my father to tell him what was going on. Like a truly supportive dad, he reassured me that he will do all he can to make this easier for me. Equally, my cousin who I was staying with, rallied around me and comforted me through it.

My dad called the lawyer and instructed him to look into ways around this. The lawyer informed us that unfortunately, in Nigeria, my hands were tied. But I did have the option of waiting a few more months and then filing in the UK. It was outside of his jurisdiction so he couldn't be my legal representative.

I didn't want to have to do this, but I had no choice and I was ready. However, there was one problem; I didn't have the marriage certificate.

When we got married, I left the marriage certificate with Joseph.

With this new information, I realised I had nothing to lose in trying; so I attempted to get a copy of the certificate.

My lawyers went to the register's office in Lagos. On his arrival, he met with the registry manager to request an additional copy of the marriage certificate. The registry was happy to provide an additional copy on the one condition that my 'husband' sign a document to give his consent for a new copy. It didn't matter that the situation was already volatile.

When I heard this news, it felt like we were back at square one. I am a woman and according to Nigerian law, my rights are different to that of my 'husband's'.

My lawyer suggested the he ask Joseph the certificate.

I had little hope that he would agree to hand the certificate over.

My lawyers contacted Joseph's lawyers and requested for the certificate. As suspected, they were reluctant to give the certificate over for reasons they never made clear. He finally agreed to send a scanned copy by email but refused to send the hard copy.

A scanned copy was of no use to me. Every lawyer I spoke to told me the same thing: without the original marriage certificate, I can't file. Seething at the series of events, I hit a dead end.

He had made it clear that there was no urgency for him to serve me with these papers, I couldn't get a copy of the certificate and there was no way a British court of law would let me file without one.

***

I knew everything I had gotten over the last year: the depression, the anxiety attacks, the feeling of worthlessness, to name a few; I was determined not to allow this situation to take me back there.

I once heard someone say 'what someone does to you is on them. But healing is your responsibility.'

Underneath the rage of what was going on with the annulment was a woman who needed to heal. More than anything, this situation showed me that I can't just say I trust God, I must show I trust Him through my actions; I have to actually leave it in His hands and let Him take control of the situation.

With nothing myself or my lawyer could do, I left it to God.

I was not sure how God would do it, but I knew that He was the only One who could.

It was time for me to continue focusing on my healing.

SCENE NINETEEN:
HEALING TIME

As time goes by, I wonder how I kept believing. How I knew I would be okay. And honestly there is only one reason. I knew that if I had to go through this, God had already given me what it takes to get through this storm gracefully. So that's what I did. I went into each new day with a new grace.

One day it was the grace not to be bitter and another it was the grace not to cuss someone out. And boy, oh boy, was my mouth ripe and ready to lay in some unforgiving insults. All in all, it was God's grace that kept me going and His mercy that kept me living.

After everything I went through, I understood why many who have been hurt by love in the past fear future relationships. I didn't know that a blow that was not physical, could cause an ache that left me breathless. I was wounded in ways that people could not see or even possibly imagine. There were days I felt as if I was dying. Days where my body would tremble at night whilst I could feel my heart rate increasing rapidly and beads of sweat rolling down my face.

Getting through that took grace and the truth is, if I knew that love could make me feel this way, I would have said no thank you and been content doing life the very same way I came into it. Alone.

I am by no means saying that I was naive to heartbreak. But that is not the side of love we so often see. We scroll through our social media and we see another couple posing for a cute soon to be viral *lovey dovey* picture.

There was no one for me to look at for examples on how to get over this level of heartbreak because this was not the kind of love that people shared.

But there was something about going back to the faithfulness of God and looking back at each challenge I had overcome throughout my life. None felt quite as painful as this, but they all ended with the same testimony. God kept me.

It was hard to be bitter when I could only think about overcoming. The present was too painful so casting my mind on it and dwelling mentally on the pain was not a constructive use of my heart or my time. Instead I would daydream about the reward. I didn't know what exactly it would be, but I knew for God to take me out of this, something better was in the pipeline. From daydreaming about the reward, I began to pray about it. I began to live life preparing for it. I gave a new relevance to my present. One that didn't involve snotty tissues and blank stares.

Of course, there were multiple hiccups on the way. Days where the prize felt too far and my heart felt so heavy. Days where I would hear his name and for a split second go back to the broken girl of April 4th 2016. But ultimately, I was focussed.

One year had passed and I had transitioned into a place I was content with. I was in a good place career wise, a few months into my blog and I was even open to dating again.

I went from hurt by love to being open to it again! I mean isn't God great. Things were still ongoing with the annulment so, of course, dating was not my focus. But the fact that the pain of my last relationship didn't turn me in the CEO of 'All Men Are Trash" association was worth celebrating. Things were certainly on the up.

But then suddenly, I found myself going back to the sleepless nights, bed sweats and the 'what ifs'. It was not long before it became apparent that I was suffering from what the doctors referred to as post traumatic anxiety. I mean, it's been a year of what I would call remarkable breakthroughs, so how could I be here?

It was only until saying the 3rd congratulations that it all became clear. I was congratulating my loved ones for new blessings. This wasn't the stage of having to attend weddings immediately after mine was cancelled. I did not have the luxury of waiting one year for that. Try one month. These congratulations were different. I was congratulating my loved ones on the blessing of pregnancy. People who said 'I do' around the time we were supposed to get married were now expanding their families. And then it occurred to me that according to our plan, I would be 3 months pregnant by now.

Me and one of my best friends would have had our babies around the same time, raised them together and got on our husband's nerves with all the matching outfits and 101 selfies until we got the magic picture. This was the plan.

While this was her reality, it was not mine. Instead, I was here, single and dealing with the ramifications of a failed love.

No one could give me a step to step 'how to' with this stage because there was no way to explain how in the midst of my genuine happiness for those I love, I was somehow reminded that things didn't work out the way I planned.

I knew I had to nip this feeling in the bud before it consumed me, so I confronted it and reminded myself of why this was best and how God works in seasons and my harvest was coming.

Combined with the uncertainty of the annulment, I grew afraid. Afraid that my life would not progress in the way I desired for myself. I wondered if I would ever have a family of my own.

What if no one would accept me and the things I had been through?

What if Joseph never sent the papers?

What if I never found love?

It was a daily battle to remind myself that all that happened did not define me, but it would build me. I had no emotional desire to be with Joseph and all this really was, was me holding on to the plans. Plans that we had not established, yet there was such an emotional attachment to the home we never lived in, the businesses we never launched and the children we never had.

"Many are the plans in the mind of a man, but it is the purpose of the Lord that will stand" Proverbs 19:21 (ESV)

I decided to live life according to a purpose. That was God's purpose for me. So even though I had all of these great plans, and boy oh boy did I plan, God's purpose would always win. In order for me to be truly happy for anyone, I had to work on the things inside of me that made someone else's happiness a reminder of my pain.

I realised that the 'What if's' were a distraction. The enemy wanted me to doubt God and His ability to restore all that I had lost. Even when emotions of 'what if' hit hard, I never stopped celebrating my loved ones. That is what my heart truly wanted to do. The logical thoughts attached to my past life with Joseph only had as much power as I gave them. So I relinquished that power and loved harder. I affirmed myself of who I was in Christ and what type of friend I needed to be. In only a matter of time, the self-pity stopped. The funk was short lived but had certainly lived long enough for me to know that I never wanted to be back here.

Fortunately, I never dealt with the fear of never having my own family again. But the anxiety about when the annulment would be over persisted.

Dear Anxiety,

You have stolen so many seconds, minutes, hours, days, weeks and months of my life.

You've made me believe that waiting in fear, anticipating the worst and wondering when, is the norm.

Instead of a half cup full, I've been drinking from a half cup empty.

As my heart heals, I feel, and I see, my mind getting more and more sick.

When!

When will I win?

When will I wake up and not worry about the things I can't control?

When will I be able to say: I AM OKAY.

Oh, anxiety.

I thought depression was bad.

But this…

When did I become so hopeless? When did I become so afraid? When did I stop believing?

The answers to the 'when' start and end with you.

The moment you crept in; darkness came with you.

I can't do this anymore. I can't live a life where you control my every thought.

Trust.

Trust in the Lord my God with all my heart.

Lean.

Lean not onto your own understanding.

I have placed my trust in the wrong thing and as a result, I have leaned on you. But anxiety you aren't my God.

It may have taken me a while to realise it, but we need to break up. I choose to not let you determine the course of my days, the hours that I sleep and the food that I eat.

You, anxiety, are a lodger that has out stayed your welcome.

It is time for you to go.

Signed,
Your never returning ex.

SCENE TWENTY:
JUNE 2017

It was one year and two months since he filed.

I had grown tired of the excuses and so I stopped asking when.

Getting over the anxiety was a process. But when God eventually healed me from it, the when's no longer mattered. I made a decision to take the control away from anxiety and leave my life in God's hands.

I no longer spent my mornings waiting to hear back from him or waiting for a delivery in the post. Instead I surrendered my day to God and trusted and believed that He wouldn't let me go through anything that would not build me.

I came home from work one afternoon and when I got into my room, I saw a letter addressed to me waiting for me on my bed side table.

On it was my name and address which had been handwritten. I couldn't recognise the handwriting. I was intrigued at what the contents would be. It was a normal sized envelope, but it was bulky.

I took off my coat, sat on my bed and opened it.

On the top layer was a letter concealing what looked like a document and a few loose pieces of paper. I pulled the letter out and before I could read it, peeping out of the bundle of paper, was a white and green document. It was the marriage certificate.

I fell to my knees and I began to weep.

I didn't know why. I didn't know how. But God heard my prayers and the very man who made it clear to me that I would not get this certificate had finally sent it to me.

I could finally file for the annulment.

I can't explain the feeling of relief that took over my entire being.

It was a bittersweet moment knowing that this sheet of paper that once represented forever, was now the very sheet of paper I would use to help us access the end.

I began my search for a solicitor who would take on this case. It became apparent that this was not that easy. Many suggested that I simply go down the divorce route. Between June and September, I lost count of how many lawyers I contacted and how many times I heard 'no'.

I tried my hardest to not be discouraged as I looked at how God had set me up to have the victory. I knew the victory was close and just like all things, the closer you get to your success the harder it is.

I began to toil with the simpler and cheaper option which was to just get a divorce. But I knew that going down this route would always remind me of the marriage that ended before it started.

Three months of no luck with finding a lawyer to represent me was tough, but I had overcome many obstacles on this eighteen month journey and this was no different.

September is the time of year we hold our annual church conference. That year, the annulment was my number one prayer request. Not 'God make me rich' and 'give me a great man' (although both were highly welcome). It was for God to find a solicitor to take on my case, for Joseph to give me no problems and for a judge to find no flaw with the annulment.

As conference went on, I felt a knowing in my spirit that what I was believing for would come to pass. I did not waste any time; I resumed my search for a lawyer.

Two days into my search, I received a call from one of the firms I sent an email to the night before. They had read the overview of my situation and asked for me to come in.

Now, you have to understand that this was not just any visit! Nope, this was a £360 per hour visit. Hesitant to go into the firm and be rejected, I requested a free phone consultation with the family law partner.

It was a longshot, but I asked anyway.

The office receptionist told me she would get back to me. 30 minutes later, I got a call from the firm.

It was one of the partners.

She went through the process and asked me why I opted for an annulment and not a divorce. She was the first person to ask me in detail. After explaining this to her, she said the words I had been longing to hear, *"we can take your case"*.

I was so used to hearing 'no' that I was on the other end of the call with my mouth wide open and my eyes tightly closed. I hadn't instructed the solicitor yet, neither was this a guarantee that it will be successful, but there was so much peace in my heart that this would be it.

I booked an appointment with the solicitor and her paralegal for the following afternoon.

On arrival to the firm I could feel anxiety rising. That day, I could barely eat or concentrate. I just wanted the meeting to be over and done with. I remember getting into the lift and going up to the top floor of the building where the offices were located. I took slow strides towards the reception until I eventually made it to the front desk.

"Hi there, can I help you?" The receptionist looked me in the face with slight worry as it became ever so apparent that she was talking to someone who was physical in body but absent in mind. Before I knew it, I was rushed to the corner sofa as my body began to slumber down to the ground.

"Are you okay? Do you need some water?'

"I am fine." I eventually responded. Around the corner came another member of staff with a chilled glass of water.

I made the silly mistake of going to the meeting alone. I knew my mum would have gladly assisted me, but at this stage over a year had passed and I didn't want her to relive a memory I wanted her to forget.

After a few moments passed and my glass of water was now empty, I managed to stand up to be escorted to the conference room where I would meet the solicitor.

The room was a long room with a window peering out onto the main road. The door and the panels into the room were made of glass. I could see people walking back and forth as I looked to the left of my shoulder.

I quickly remembered that this meeting was charged by the hour and regained my focus.

The lawyer introduced herself and gave me a background of her experience and expertise. Almost like she was selling herself to me.

She then began to read my case based on the email enquiry I was asked to complete.

Hearing a complete stranger retell a snippet of my story was something I hadn't experienced before. I had barely told some of my most loved ones let alone this stranger. As she got to the last sentence and prepared to ask me to tell her the circumstances behind our breakup, I lifted the new glass of water prepared for me as my mouth suddenly became increasingly dry.

It was my turn to speak.

I started to narrate the story of events step by step trying not to leave any detail out. I planned to tell her why we broke up, why the previous filing failed and why I was filing. And 30 seconds into our conversation I began to cry. A cry I had not cried for months. A cry of deep sorrow and pain. It was almost as if in that moment, I became the heartbroken girl crying on her bedroom floor all over again.

As I continued to tell the solicitor all I had been through, she knew this case was not the typical annulment case. How would we prove to a judge that there were grounds? Would my ex cooperate? I had to have faith that the international borders, and the now lack of communication between myself and Joseph, would not deter this from going on. I knew this was it. I knew this was not going to be dragging over my head for much longer.

After hearing my side, she agreed to take my case. I knew she would from the moment she sold herself to me.

She said there was something about me that made her want me to be free. Despite knowing that my case would exceed the set hours of a normal annulment case, she gave me a fixed fee.

In that moment, I knew God orchestrated this.

For the first time in over a year, I felt the end closely approaching.

Immediately after I left the meeting, the lawyer and her team began proceedings. At every stage, they kept me informed. Something I was not use to. They contacted Joseph to tell him I was filing and served him with the papers. Within 24 hours, he responded to my solicitor with no hesitation.

Everything was going so smoothly. I often pinched myself to make sure I was not dreaming. I knew that this was God's doing. He turned hearts towards me to favour me. Even the heart of my ex which I was convinced, only a few months prior, was made of steel.

Roughly seven months after our initial consultation, the annulment was finalised.

I didn't have to prove in court that this marriage was not consummated, I didn't even have to spend the arm and the leg originally anticipated. There was no element of this that God did not take care of. God gave me the easiest 6 months that made the 18 months prior seem necessary.

I was at work when the news came in that the annulment was finalised. I remember opening the email and attached was the court ruling. I gazed at the screen for about 10 minutes reading the document over, and over, again. The moment I had been waiting for had finally arrived. I didn't know how to feel.

Two months prior, when the judge accepted the decree nisi, I cried with so much joy! I was sure that I would do the same once it was actually finalised. But I didn't. I couldn't. I just sat there in amazement that it was finished.

That night we had a service at church. It was not until I picked up the mic and began to sing that I realised just how much I had to be thankful for. I sang like never before and danced till my feet were tired. I was finally free.

SCENE TWENTY-ONE: BEAUTIFUL ENDINGS

In the months leading up to the annulment being finalised, I grew up. My trials made me stronger than ever and gave me a voice to so many people who needed it.

I didn't think that my pain would be able to bring forth light into the lives of others and hope into my own life.

Every day I never gave up, I gave God the opportunity to prove Himself as God in my life.

So many times I doubted myself for the decisions I made but I never doubted Him.

I learnt so many lessons to build me into the woman, wife and mother I know I will become. It is ironic that in this time, I learnt the true meaning of loving a spouse when I didn't have one to love. I had to learn what God intended in marital love and not just go by what I felt and the person I felt it for. I also learnt that what works for others may not work for me. For starters, long distance relationships can work but it really was not for me.

Why, you may ask. Sometimes in relationships we get to the point where we want to be with someone so badly, that we make wishes on their behalf. I say wishes because that is what it is. I wanted to change what he wanted in order to suit what I wanted.

I created my own version of the story. A version that involved tube journeys to work and not drivers. A version that consisted of snow is December and not harmattan. There were no cooks, house help or drivers. This version involved me being happy and him not. Of course, that was not my intention but when we look at it for what it was, I wanted him to do something that would make him miserable to appease my desire to remain comfortable.

It is important that we are always honest with what we want. We let it get so far without ever really discussing how we both felt about making major adjustments to our norm. Over the years, I have seen many wives and husbands relocate for the sake of their marriage. But the difference between the two of us was the 'will'.

Never assume on behalf of your partner that they are 'okay' with change. Have the difficult conversations before you get to 'I do'. If something changes along the journey, communicate this to them. We may have the Holy Spirit in us but that by no means makes us mind readers!

Being true to each other is one of the most undervalued gifts in any relationships.

In relationships, people evolve. I changed, he changed. What we wanted changed. But we remained in the years we were two love birds finding their feet instead of evolving together. If I could do anything differently, I would have never stopped the discussions. Painful or not, I would have asked the hard questions.

Eventually I realised that holding regrets on what I should or shouldn't have done, will not change it. But I can learn from it and share my lessons with others along the way.

By going behind the scenes of this snapshot of my life, I hope you see a woman not defeated by the multiple trials she encountered, but one who used God's love, her faith and determination to come out stronger.

There were two things I could control in this: what I did and how I responded to what was done to me.

Knowing God didn't stop me from making mistakes. But having an intimate relationship with Him helped me to navigate through them. It helped me to see life through the eyes of grace and not condemnation. I was so close to allowing the guilt of the mistakes I've made in this relationship rob me from moving on.

It's not easy to know that some of the errors I made could have been avoided if I simply placed God ahead of my fleshly desires. Often our guilt is our self-righteous way of making ourselves feel better. At least if I feel guilty, God will know I am sorry. I quickly learnt that all God wanted from me was to repent for placing this relationship above Him and then give Him my heart fully. Not in part, not with limitations, but completely.

I was so sure I lost myself during the process. I wasn't doing the things I use to do that reminded me of me. Every time I tried to search for who Sarah was, I hit a wall.

But by my giving my heart to God I was able to see what guilt couldn't show me.

I saw that because of the pain, I began to build a number of walls. And as these layers grew in its thickness, it became harder and harder to strip it down back to the surface. The surface being the me that appeared *lost*.

The issue was not that I was lost, it was that I couldn't recognise myself under the scars.

But the lost me was always right there. She was just waiting for me to realise that every wall and layer of pain steered my life in a new direction. And it was up to *me* to choose the destination.

The closer I got to God, the more I realised that who I am and who I will ever be is in Him.

I was so deep in the valley I had all my pain be the fuel to my growth. To sit down and dissect my past and acknowledge the points that I went wrong, and the points that I was wronged was painful. 2 out of 3 times I would give up before I started. But I was so tired of not being able to find the bubbly, happy, positive woman I used to be. I was ready to identify *her* again… better yet I wanted to get to know the refined her! So that's what I did!

I faced my pain. It was not the easiest process to dig at my lowest point. But it's when I kept digging that I was able to stop feeding the roots of the pain and put down new roots using the lessons I had learnt.

I let go of the baggage I held on to and I was able to be free. Free mentally, emotionally and creatively. I was able to channel my pain to a notepad instead of people. I was able to give my yoke to my Maker and not feed it to my mind. This is the reFINEd me!

- The refined me is stronger.
- The refined me knows better than to give up!
- She knows better than to lose faith.
- She knows that there is beauty in pain and freedom in her story!
- She is and will forever be a product and giver of love
- The refined me found out that even a romantic like myself

can see that my hurt was not the end but a 'to be continued' to a better future

The refined me knows that her best is yet to come.

ABOUT THE AUTHOR

Sarah Alonge is a London based public speaker, writer and minister. She is passionate about building fruitful and purposeful relationships. Her testimony has helped a vast number of people across the world overcome the consequences of dysfunctional relationships through helping them to see their identity in Christ and that they are more than what they have been through.

You can connect with Sarah at www.sarahalonge.com

Printed in Great Britain
by Amazon

62516973R00087